IMMANUEL BIRMELIN

My
Parakeet

BARRON'S

CONTENTS

1 Typical Parakeets

7 **Getting to Know These Little Parrots**

7 The Wild Ancestors
9 Parakeets as Pets
10 ▸ **Did You Know That . . .** parakeets were once considered delicacies?
11 Biological Profile
13 **Tip:** How to avoid behavioral disorders
14 Sexing Parakeets
14 Sensory Capabilities
15 **Table:** Differences between wild parakeets and captive-bred varieties
15 With the Eyes of a Parakeet
16 **Tip:** Getting to know the world of senses
17 With the Ears of a Parakeet
17 Sense of Smell
18 Sense of Taste
18 Vibratory Sense

19 This Is How Parakeets Live
20 From Necessity to Virtue
22 Behavior Patterns: Look Closely!
22 What Your Parakeets Are Trying to "Tell" You
22 Clues to the Body Language of Parakeets
24 ▸ **My pet: Getting to know your parakeets**
24 Having Other Parakeets Around Is Important
25 All About Compatibility
25 There Must Be Order: Classification of Parakeets

27 **Popular Color Varieties**

27 Beauty Contest
27 **Tip:** Parakeet show standards
28 Portraits of Parakeet Breeds— at a Glance

2 How Parakeets Like to Live

35 **A Home to Feel Comfortable in**

35 Lots of Room in a Comfortable Parakeet Home
36 The Right Place for the Parakeet Home
37 **Checklist:** Free-flight Dangers
38 The Basic Home
39 ▸ **Did you know that . . .** birds can fly very fast?
39 Functional Cage Furnishings
40 The Importance of Play
41 Basic Cage Furnishings—at a Glance

43 **Exercise Is Always Good**

43 Please, Keep in Mind!
44 The Outdoor Aviary
46 Aviary Furnishings
46 **Tip:** A room for birds in your home
46 Parakeets Must Fly
48 The Climbing Tree
48 ▸ **My pet: What are your parakeets' favorite toys?**

Welcome Home

51 **Purchase and Selection of Parakeets**
51 Where Do You Find Your Feathered Friends?
52 **Checklist:** Healthy Parakeets
54 ▶ **Parents' Extra:** Not Interested in Parakeets
55 Age at the Time of Purchase
55 Distinguishing the Sexes
55 My Personal View About Your Purchase Choice

56 **Settling In … Gently**
56 Your Empathy Is Needed

57 Transporting Your Birds Home … Gently
58 The Parakeets in Their New Home
59 The ABC for an Effortless Adjustment
59 **Tip:** Taking care of the birds during the first few days
61 Taming Parakeets
61 ▶ **Did you know that …** not every parakeet is a gifted "talker"?
62 ▶ **My pet:** "daredevil" or "chicken-hearted"?
64 Questions on Maintenance and Settling In

Nutrition

67 **Correct Nutrition— an Important Subject**
67 Male Parakeets Remain Slim
68 ▶ **Did you know that …** juvenile birds already have food preferences?
69 What Do Wild Parakeets Feed On?
70 Seeds as Staple Food
71 Healthy Diet—at a Glance

72 **Nutritional Building Blocks**
72 Protein Ensures Renewal
72 Carbohydrates Provide the Fuel
73 Fat—Sheer Energy
74 Minerals Ensure Well-being
74 **Table:** Diet plan for your parakeets
75 Vitamins Are Essential for the Metabolism
76 Green Feed Is Part of the Diet Plan

77 Dinner Is Served
77 **Checklist:** Feeding Rules
78 ▶ **My pet:** Food preferences of your parakeet
78 Nibbling Food
78 Something Tasty for In-between
79 The Right Drink
79 Toxic and Dangerous

5 Well Cared-for and Perfectly Happy

81 Cleanliness Is the First Commandment

81 Preening—An Important Matter
82 Caring for Your Birds
83 Cage Maintenance
83 Cleaning the Aviary
83 **Tip:** Injury while trimming the claws
84 ▸ Parents' Extra: Saying Good-bye
85 The Molt
86 ▸ My pet: Is your parakeet maintaining its weight?

87 Common Diseases

87 "Difficult" Patients
87 How to Recognize Disease Symptoms
88 Skin and Feather Diseases

90 Viral Diseases
91 Inflammation of the Crop
91 Parrot Disease (*Psittacosis*)
91 Going-light Syndrome (GLS)
91 ▸ Did you know that . . .
    parakeet feathers are continuously replaced?
92 Abscesses and Tumors
92 This Is What You Can Do
93 Administering Medication
93 **Checklist:** First Aid Kit for Parakeets
94 Questions: All About Parakeet Care and Health

6 Activities and Learning

97 Special Training for Parakeets

97 Learn for Life While Playing
98 Games that Provide Fun and Stimulate Thinking
99 Adventure Playground
99 Parakeets Must Never Be Bored
100 Parakeets Enjoy Learning
101 ▸ Did you know that . . .
    every parakeet has a distinctive personality?
102 Things Parakeets Learn Easily
104 **Table:** Toys preferred by parakeets

105 Misjudged Geniuses

105 "Masked Ball" in the Parakeet Aviary
106 A Surprisingly Good Memory

106 Brainy "Heads"
107 **Checklist:** Learning per a Study Program
108 Talented "Talkers"
109 The Art of Imitation
109 **Tip:** "Speech" lessons
110 Creative Thinking
110 ▸ My pet: How to improve your parakeets' intelligence

New Arrivals in the Parakeet Home

113 **"Family Planning" for Parakeets**

113 What to Do With the Progeny?
113 Healthy Parents
114 ▶ **Did you know that . . .** parakeet mothers help their young?
114 Basic Building Blocks of Genetics
116 **Tip:** Size of the Entrance Hole
116 Important for Breeding
118 Partner Selection, Courtship, and Mating
118 **Tip:** It must not be too warm

120 **Healthy and Happy**

120 The Time Before Hatching
121 Difficult "Birth"
121 Development of the Young
122 The Development—at a Glance
123 The Chicks Are Discovering the World
124 Care of the Young
124 ▶ **My pet: How considerate are parakeet parents?**
125 Once Breeding Is Over
125 Time to Say Good-bye to the Young

What to Do When There Are Problems

127 **How to Solve Husbandry (Keeping) Problems Correctly**

127 Courting the Mirror
128 Can a Single Bird Also Be Happy?
128 The Parakeet Refuses Green Feed
128 When the Leg Has Swollen Because of the Leg Band
128 Parakeets Mourn the Loss of Their Partners
129 ▶ **Did you know that . . .** a parakeet can get lost?

130 When the Parakeets Are Getting Old
131 The Parakeet Mother Has Died
131 Intruders in the Nest Box
132 Getting Used to Each Other
133 "Perpetual Breeders"
133 Learning to "Talk"
133 **Tip:** Hand-reared birds
133 Your Parakeet Has Escaped
134 ▶ **My pet: How do parakeets spend their day?**
136 Pet-sitter Checklist

Appendix

138 Index
141 Resources
142 Picture credits
144 Copyright

Typical Parakeets

They are the most popular pet birds in the world . . . and not without reason. It is not only their pretty appearance that fascinates us, but also their intelligence and their charming nature.

Getting to Know These Little Parrots

Take to a journey to Australia, to the country of the wild parakeets.
Go on a search for the roots of your feathered housemates with all their interesting
behaviors and abilities.

Millions of blue, yellow, green, and colorfully mottled parakeets live in the care of humans. Breeders have combined the genetic characteristics of our feathered friends into spectacular color variations and bizarre mutations. As pets, parakeets have become more colorful, but also heavier and more portly than their wild ancestors have. In the Australian wilderness, our pet parakeets would no longer be able to survive.

The Wild Ancestors

Appearance: A wild parakeet (about sparrow size) weighs approximately 1 ounce (30 g), but our domestic parakeets now weigh generally in excess of 1.75 ounces (50 g). The "wild" cousin has a predominantly green or greenish plumage. The wings and back are blackish brown. Their head is yellow with dense black striped markings; the face (mask) is bright yellow from the crown down to the throat. The attractive, violet cheek patches contain three black dots each around the throat. The tail feathers are very long. The parakeet is an attractive, elegant bird that can withstand the difficult living conditions of the Australian continent, especially the harsh climate and the lack of rain. Wild parakeets roam through dry areas in the center of the continent where it rarely rains. These efficient flyers migrate over thousands of miles in search of water. During these journeys, hundreds of thousands birds will perish. Sometimes it can take months, even years, for precipitation to reach these arid regions. As soon as the first raindrops fall, the birds look for caves and commence—as if given a starting signal—with mating, laying eggs, and rearing their young. In quick succession, they will rear several broods with up to eight young, and so make up for high mortalities during the

A clean plumage guarantees an efficient flight. These parakeets are taking the task of cleaning their plumage very seriously.

drought period. Although it never rains for very long, the precipitation is sufficient to establish new plant growth, flowering, and fruit development within a very short period. Male parakeets, which provide the food—initially for the female in the nesting cave and then for the growing family—find sufficient seeds, even long after the rainwater has evaporated.

Life in a flock: The wild, green parakeets never live alone. They congregate into huge flocks, sometimes up to thousands of birds. The advantage of life in a flock is obvious: Food and water is easier to find when in a large group, and mutual protection can be provided through appropriate warning sounds. When the birds are threatened, they emit a characteristic warning call and the entire flock takes off immediately. Birds of prey, such as peregrine falcons, find it difficult to single out an individual bird in flight. It is hard to focus on an individual when the entire flock seems like a single unit. In a flock, one bird has to learn what the other birds are doing. Therefore, it is no surprise that parakeets are excellent observers and always look at the other birds around them. That applies not only to wild parakeets but also to those kept as pets. For instance, if flying parakeets see others that are feeding, they will join in and the entire flock will get larger and larger. You can observe this very same behavior in your own birds. If a small group of them or an individual settles to the

1 **Outlook** From a high vantage point, such a tree is not only suited for resting, but also as a vantage point to look for lucrative feeding grounds or a watering hole.

2 **Finally . . . water** In their native Australia, parakeets' lives are constantly threatened by extensive drought periods. Water is essential for their survival, and when a watering hole is found, the birds will drink and bathe to the fullest.

This male parakeet feeds his female, ▶
so that she can feed the brood
inside the nesting cave.

ground in search of food, the others will quickly follow.

Joint cause: Parakeets do nearly everything together. No bird will go off on its own. Even during the midday rest period, hundreds of birds perch in the cool shade of trees. When the temperatures rise above 95°F (35°C) the birds will spread their wings slightly and open their beaks. This provides cooling for the body. My birds will do the same on a hot summer day. There is much joy among my parakeets when they get an artificial rain shower. To do that, I spray water from a garden hose against the roof of my large aviary, so that it drips down like rain. It is a marvelous shower pleasure for the birds.

These small birds are particularly resilient and real survivors. At a temperature of 38°F (20°C) and a humidity of 30 percent, parakeets can survive up to 30 days without drinking a single drop of water. That is an unbelievable achievement, and it is very hard to imagine that such a small body can endure it. This has never been tested experimentally and you must NEVER try it out on your birds. We must look for the answer in the evolutionary process. Everything in parakeets is designed to economize on the use of water. Water is scarce in their natural habitat, and so these birds will remain almost motionless in the shade of trees during the hottest part of the day. Movements cause an increase in oxygen consumption, which in turn increases respiratory (lung) activity, which then

causes increased evaporation of body moisture. In essence, then, parakeets have become optimally adapted to nature through their behavior.

Parakeets as Pets

The joint history of humans and parakeets is young compared with that of dogs or cats with humans. We have known of the existence of these elegant little birds for only about 200 years. The first description is by Shaw and Nodder in 1805. Parakeets were introduced into Europe by the British natural scientist John Gould. He traveled with his wife throughout Australia, and discovered these fast, green birds in the heart of the continent. Gould was excited about them and observed their mode of life in detail. His results are published in the book *Birds of Australia.* What John Gould encapsulated in words, his wife documented with very attractive drawings. Her pictures are alive with spectacular, minute details. Hardly anybody has ever been able to draw these birds as precisely as she did. John Gould gave parakeets the scientific name *Melopsittacus undulates* (Shaw). *Nomen est Omen* is a Latin saying that means "the

Nowadays, parakeets are the most popular pet birds in the world. Their triumphant march began during the nineteenth century, when returning settlers brought them to Europe. As early as 1880 an exhibition was held near Toulouse, where 15,000 birds were exhibited. The popularity of parakeets is most certainly because of their appearance, but to me even more important is their nature. They are easy to train, friendly, sociable, and have the ability to talk. The first parakeet in Europe that was known to talk babbled its sentence

DID YOU KNOW THAT . . .

. . . parakeets were once considered delicacies?

The original inhabitants of Australia, the aborigines, gave parakeets the name *Betcherrygah*, which translates roughly into "good meal." Incidentally, this term also led to the English name *budgerigar* for the parakeet. Budgerigars and parakeets are the same, but in North America they are more commonly known as parakeets. The Aborigines appreciated the little parrot as a delicacy. These birds made it particularly easy for people to obtain a tasty meal. Under optimal environmental conditions, parakeets breed in large aggregations, up to hundreds of birds at the same time. They nest in tree hollows, where the young hatch from eggs. During their development, the young poke their heads out of the nesting cave nearly always at the same time, to beg for food from their parents. Therefore, the Aborigines only needed to reach up into parakeet nesting caves and they had a full meal.

name is an omen." That truly applies to parakeets. *Melos* is Greek and means "song"; *psittacus* is also Greek and means "parrot." *Undulatus* is the Latin word for "wave line" and refers to wave-like markings on the plumage. The name Shaw refers to the original discoverer of the parakeet.

in German. One morning in 1877, Mrs. E. Mayer in Stuttgart, Germany was greeted by her parakeet with the words "Come, darling, come." The surprise felt by the woman must have been immense. The speech talent of these small parrots was well rewarded. Periodically, one bird would fetch as much as $1,000.

Some of the most important elements in the life of a parakeet are **companionship** and **mental stimulation**. The human cannot be a substitute for a bird partner, so when only keeping one parakeet, it's important to provide a lot of attention.

Parakeets Provide Quality of Life

Parakeets enrich the lives around them. It is well known that pets have a positive effect on children. It has now been scientifically proven that parakeets also provide a better quality of life for older people. One hundred occupants in various nursing homes were given parakeets to look after. The result after only eight weeks was extraordinary. The "bird sitters" enjoyed life more and their contacts with the other home occupants had improved. These elderly people had much to say about their experiences and adventures with the birds. The life of those seniors had been given new meaning.

Biological Profile

Skeleton: The hollow bones (not filled with bone marrow) are particularly lightweight. Their component of the total body weight is only about 8 to 9 percent. The lightweight construction of the skeleton is already an indicator that parakeets are excellent flyers by nature. In the pelvic region, there are the lumbar, sacral, and first caudal vertebrae, which have become fused into a compact bone that provides a strong support apparatus for the body of the bird. At the end of the vertebral column, there is a coccygeal bone. At the breast-bone (sternum), there is the origin of the flight muscles. The large eye sockets are conspicuous. The upper and lower beaks are hinged to the skeleton. Each foot has four toes, which are linked to the leg by means of the metatarsophalangeal joint. Two toes are pointing forward and two are pointing backward.

Body weight: It seems that the average body weight of our parakeet has increased during the last decades. Reliable measurements during the 1970s indicate a weight of about 1.4 ounce (40 g). Birds weighed in 2005 revealed a weight of 1.5 ounce (50 g). Presumably, this increase is caused by long-term captive breeding.

Wonderful! A bath in a flowerpot saucer.

1 **Grooming** the plumage is a very important task for parakeets. However, anyone choosing a rolling ball while doing that job has to do a bit of a balancing act.

2 Initially, **the balancing act** works rather well. The feathers are meticulously pulled through the beak.

3 **Then the ball rolls** and everything collapses. Fortunately, a parakeet can fly—if it had been us, we would certainly have crash-landed.

Age: A healthy parakeet can reach an age of 12 to 14 years.

Body temperature: On the average, this is 100°F (42.1°C). With a body temperature of 104.9°F (40.5°C), one talks about hypothermia. We would already have a high fever at that temperature. At 109°F (42.6°C), parakeets only have a fever, but we would generally already be dead.

Musculature: The two pectoral muscles, which move the wings up and down, weigh nearly as much as all the other muscles together (about $\frac{1}{3}$ ounce [11 g]). This number clearly indicates how important it is that the pectoral muscles be used daily during free flight (see Parakeets Must Fly, page 46).

Heart: The average weight of the parakeet heart is .58 g; it is 14.1 mm long and 7.5 mm wide. Relating this to the total body mass of a parakeet of 1.4 ounce (40 g), means it is 1.2 percent of the body mass. How large this percentage figure really is can be seen in a comparison with the human heart. In a human of 154 pounds (70 kg) body weight the heart weighs about 11 ounces (300 g), which expressed as percentage body weight, is only .4 percent. The heart of a parakeet beats 300 to 500 times a minute. How breathtakingly fast this really is, you can check yourself. Try tapping the table with your finger 500 times a minute. That is almost impossible.

Only 6 ml of blood flow in the blood vessels of parakeets—no more than a drop. No high-performance athlete has such a heavy, high-capacity heart in comparison to his body mass. The heart of the parakeet is a real powerhouse.

Respiratory system: Birds have the most efficient respiratory system of all animals. Their lungs are built according to a different structural system than those of mammals. Their lungs are connected to air sacs. Such a system has two advantages: First, the air taken in can be better used, that is, the amount of oxygen per breath is greater than in our lungs. Second, it makes flying easier. Parakeets

require a lot of oxygen. Therefore, the room where their cage is in your house needs to be well ventilated.

Digestive system: Whatever part of the parakeet's anatomy we look at, it is all well adapted so that these birds can fly easily. That includes the digestive system.

Before food reaches the stomach, it first passes through the crop. The crop is an enlargement of the esophagus and serves as a food container and preparation area for the actual digestive process in the stomach. In order to avoid the need to carry around unnecessary weight, the stomach is filled only when the crop is already full.

From the stomach the macerated food passes into the small intestine, large intestine, and then into the rectum. The last segment of the rectum forms the cloaca, which is also known as the vent. This is the opening where both feces and urine exit the bird. In males, it is also where the delivery tube for sperm meets with the female's cloaca, which

receives it for fertilization. Birds have only this single opening for the discharge of excrement and eggs. The entire length of the intestine, from its origin at the stomach to the cloaca, measures 8½ inches (21.5 cm).

TIP

How to avoid behavioral disorders

Parakeets have many innate types of behavior. If they are prevented from using them, they might develop behavioral disorders. By their very nature, parakeets thrive on the acoustic and optical presence of a parakeet partner. Although a single bird can be kept happily and healthily if it receives a lot of attention, you might consider purchasing two birds if you will be away most of the day and cannot offer a consistent amount of attention.

Sexing Parakeets

Who is who? The answer to this question is important when keeping parakeets, because female parakeets among themselves are sometimes rather unfriendly. For that reason, I advise you to keep only one female within any group of parakeets (see All About

In order to understand parakeets you must get involved in the character of these little parrots.

Compatibility, page 25). In adult birds, the sexes are easy to distinguish. Upon completion of the juvenile molt, the featherless skin, or *cere*, of the nose area above the beak changes color. In males, it turns blue, and in females, it becomes brownish beige. With juvenile birds, even experienced breeders and bird

dealers often have difficulty determining the sex, because this skin is light pink or light beige in males as well as in females. A helpful hint: Hens have hair-thin, light-colored to whitish rings around their nostrils.

However, one can be sure only when the bird is older and male and female hormones are fully active. There are even more confusing aspects here: In older males (generally those older than seven years), the blue cere becomes discolored to a brownish beige. Why is that?

In older birds, the levels of female hormones increase. This may sound strange, but it is quite natural within the normal biological development of these birds. Even in humans, the hormone concentration changes in older people. Following menopause in females, the male hormonal levels increase. So, why do female hormones increase in birds and male hormones in mammals? The arrangement of sex chromosomes in males and females is different in mammals and birds. In mammals, the male carries one X- and one Y-chromosome (see page 116) and females carry two X-chromosomes. In birds, the cocks have two X-chromosomes and the hens one X- and one Y–chromosome.

Parakeets are flying acrobats. Therefore, as pets they require a lot of supervised ◀ free-flight time.

Sensory Capabilities

People who want to look after their birds properly must enter into a "dialogue of senses" with them. Bird owners who do not know that their protégés can see more colors or can perceive different tones than humans, will certainly make mistakes when caring for them. Every sensory organ in every animal species, whether eye or ear, has been adapted to the environment in the

DIFFERENCES BETWEEN WILD PARAKEETS AND CAPTIVE-BRED VARIETIES

THEY DIFFER PRINCIPALLY IN THEIR APPEARANCE

Wild form	Captive-bred variety
Plumage: light to dark green color; face and forehead (mask) bright yellow; six black spots around throat and chest; blue violet cheek patches; wavelike markings along nape, back, and top of wings.	**Plumage:** There are now many color varieties and variable plumage colors and markings
Size: 6 to 8 inches (16–20 cm)	**Size:** often larger than 8 inches (20 cm) (according to standard: 8½ inches [21.6 cm] and larger)
Weight: app. 1 ounce (30 g)	**Weight:** 1 to 1.75 ounce (30–50 g) and more

course of the evolutionary process. For instance, elephants can perceive sounds that remain hidden from our ears, but are essential for the life of the elephants. Females in estrus calling out for males that are many miles away use infrasound. When this was discovered about 25 years ago, it was a sensation. Since then zoos have been using this capability in their elephant husbandry programs. I wish this would also happen for parakeets.

Sensory organs are the gateways to the outside world, which is perceived differently by each animal species. Unfortunately, many who keep animals underestimate the significance of this for the well-being of an animal species,

or may even totally ignore it. These people see animals with their eyes and then transfer their own perspective to that of the animals. This can lead to completely wrong conclusions. If one could ask a parakeet—and indeed, if the bird could answer —how he liked the latest Harry Potter film, the bird's answer would be clear and unambiguous. It had not seen a film, only a slow-moving slide lecture (see With the Eyes of a Parakeet, below).

With the Eyes of a Parakeet

Bird eyes are the largest among vertebrate animals (birds, fish, amphibians, reptiles, and mammals), relatively speaking. Their head volume is about

50 percent of the entire body volume, which is in contrast to only 5 percent in humans. These numbers speak for themselves, and indicate where the strength of birds lies: in their vision. The laterally located eyes give the parakeet nearly complete all-round visibility. Therefore, even enemies that approach from behind have hardly any chance to stay unrecognized. Birds see the largest part of their surroundings one dimensionally, with only one eye. In fact, they are even able to adjust the eyes independently to different focal distances. Their eyes can also move independently. For instance, starlings are able to check the ground area around the beak with one eye and monitor the sky above with the other. Whether parakeets have similar capabilities has—to my knowledge—not yet been scientifically investigated. I believe that parakeets are not an exception to that. I continue to be amazed at the details my birds notice in their aviary. They can see every bird of prey in the sky and at the same time observe the activities on the ground. Many birds of prey have excellent spatial (i.e, three-dimensional) vision. A bird that wants to capture its prey in midair must know the distance to the prey. To estimate intervals correctly requires spatial vision. Therefore, how and what an animal sees is dependent upon the living conditions. The spatial vision in parakeets is probably only limited. These birds live in a colorful world: Their eyes are far better at distinguishing colors than our own. The human eye contains three types of light-sensitive cells, which absorb red, green, and blue light. Our brain manipulates millions of color impressions. Color television sets work according to a similar principle. Parakeets have four types of sensory cells. The fourth one absorbs ultraviolet radiation from sunlight. Recently, it was learned that these birds also perceive fluorescent light. The discovery of this ability makes for an exciting story, and this much can be said: It plays an important role in the selection of a partner.

Parakeets' eyes process 150 images per second, which means that their eyes can process movement sequences in up to 150 individual images per second. On the other hand, humans can manage only a modest 15 to 20 images per second.

Parakeets' process images at time-lapse speed and can therefore better detect the movements of their enemies. What needs to be kept in mind here for the husbandry of parakeets is their reaction to neon light, which I describe in Chapter 2 on page 36. For instance, it is interesting to know how birds react when given the choice of a light or a dark room.

TIP

Getting to know the world of senses

When you know how parakeets perceive their surroundings, you can avoid dangers. For instance, the birds usually see a large glass pane only when it is already too late. Their spatial vision is significantly less developed than ours. In addition, noise often triggers fear and panic among parakeets.

Curious and clever: That is ▶
precisely what a parakeet is.

With the Ears of a Parakeet

General noise as well as particular sounds, tones, and singing play a significant role in the world of parakeets. Throughout their lives, they learn new sounds, and there is a very good reason for that. Sound utterances serve as social communication. Male parakeets have a repertoire of contact calls, some of which even strengthen the pair bond. Similarly, in their relationship to humans, sounds play a significant role. After all, parakeets are able to mimic human speech, so it does not come as a surprise to learn that they can hear very well.

The ears are hidden under plumage behind the eyes. External ears are absent—they would only be superfluous ballast for these little flyers. For a long time it was believed that, because of their small heads, it was difficult for parakeets to distinguish sounds originating from different locations. There was a lot of support for the belief that their directional hearing was not particularly well developed, but science has since contradicted this assumption. The directional hearing of parakeets is nearly as good as that of humans. In fact, their sense of hearing is barely different from our own. The lower audible limit for parakeets is around 40 Hz and the upper limit around 14,000 Hz (in humans it is 16 Hz to 20,000 Hz). Our ear is the most sensitive to sounds of 2,000 Hz; for other frequencies, we need to speak more loudly so that we are understood. The ears of parakeets are also the most sensitive within the frequency range of 2,000 Hz to 4,000 Hz. However, in one respect parakeets are ahead of us. They are able to resolve acoustic signals faster than we can. Parakeets perceive as a recognizable tone sequence (that they can repeat unchanged) what is, for us, nothing more than quick screeching. Their acoustic memory is superb and they can easily memorize certain frequencies. This ensures survival, because the alarm call must never be adulterated.

Sense of Smell

Generations of scientists believed that birds are unable to smell. This is understandable, because we never see or hear birds sniffing. Consequently, it is easy to assume that birds are unable to smell. However, that opinion seems to be changing. In the meantime, it has been

Want to talk? Even parakeets sometimes have differences of opinion. Apparently, there is a serious discussion in progress here. Will there be an agreement?

discovered that some bird species are capable of smelling. Whether parakeets can smell is—to the best of my knowledge—still unknown. My many years of experience do not provide any suggestion, one way or the other. I am of the opinion that smell plays only a very small part (if one at all) in the life of these little parrots.

Sense of Taste

How well parakeets can taste has not yet been scientifically investigated. We have to rely principally on the observations of bird hobbyists. Many parakeets are allowed to nibble on the food eaten by their owners, and so have displayed certain preferences for one or the other type of food. This suggests taste preferences. Their close relatives, the large parrot species, have 350 taste buds on their tongues (humans have 9,000); presumably, parakeets have the same number as large parrots. Their behavior

suggests that there are preferences. Whatever does not taste good is spat out in a manner suggesting nausea, accompanied by vigorous head shaking.
Tip: Strongly seasoned food can damage the health of your parakeets. Also, foods like chocolate or avocado, and drinks containing caffeine or alcohol are dangerous for parakeets. Therefore your birds should not be given food from your table.

Vibratory Sense

The vibration center of parakeets is in their legs. Just like a seismograph, the vibratory center registers every movement of the ground or substrate. This sensitivity to vibrations should be taken into account when selecting the cage: If it is not free of vibrations, the occupants can easily panic. Therefore, never place the cage on something like a vibrating refrigerator—not even for a few minutes.

This Is How Parakeets Live

Parakeets live in flocks. Within such flocks, there are small groups or pairs. Once a male and female have come together as a pair, they are permanently monogamous. This can easily be observed by anyone who keeps several birds. Like two lovers, the pair will bill and coo, picking at each other's plumage and flying jointly on exploratory trips: There is no doubt that these two are a pair. If this is followed by successfully raising young from a clutch of eggs, the two will remain together for their entire lives. This "marital vitality" has been scientifically investigated by the biologist Fritz Trillmich. After a separation of 70 days, a pair continued to bill and coo just like before. During the interim period, each partner of the pair lived separately with siblings of the same sex. Trillmich conducted many controlled experiments. One of these showed that a separation of 20 days had no influence on pair bonding, although the partners had opportunity during the period of separation to become attached to other sex partners. What Trillmich determined scientifically, I have often observed with my birds, and this fidelity between partners has always fascinated me.

There is one story that I shall never forget and that touches me to this day. Max and Susie were an inseparable pair that had formed within my group of birds. One day Susie became ill. She sat quietly on a perch, with fluffed-up feathers. I reached for my special remedy, an infrared heat lamp, which I installed in such a way that Susie could select the distance to the warming beam herself. The next day I did not believe

my eyes. Max, the male, had moved closely to Susie and put his wing "lovingly" around her, a touching scene that I have witnessed repeatedly since then. Such close pair bonding has, of course, practical consequences.

Experts in matters "nibbling"

▶ **1** **The beak** has the same meaning for parakeets as hands have for humans. Everything is closely examined using the beak.

▶ **2** **Nibbling** on branches and leaves provides the bird with minerals, satisfies the gnawing instinct, and keeps the birds busy for hours. Gnawing material should always be made available to parakeets.

A pair should never be separated unless there is a valid reason. I am quite convinced that these birds fret or even mourn for a lost partner. Max and Susie started me thinking, and I wanted to know how strong pair bonding within individual pairs really is. A year and a half of scientific drudgery lay ahead of me. It involved daily, exact recording of

Birds that have formed a pair must never be separated. They will mourn the loss of their partner.

behavior observations, which is hard, sometimes even mind-numbing, work.

I noted that certain pairs would sit together more frequently and were more often engaged in preening each other and mutual billing. This was not really amazing, however; what was surprising was the fact that pairs, which preened and billed each other more frequently also copulated more frequently—but (as must be noted here) not for reproductive purposes. Birds that preened each other less never did this. Obviously, some of my parakeets are more "affectionate" than others. This also manifested itself in their being less aggressive toward each other. However, a real surprise was that compared with the less "amorous" ones, their copulations tended to last longer. This raises the interesting question of whether the more affectionate pairs are possibly producing more progeny or whether their progeny are stronger. A precise analysis revealed that this is an incorrect assumption. My birds appeared to have

feelings without biological consequences. Therefore, it makes sense that parakeets enter into pair bonds of variable strengths. This underlines how important other members of the same species are for these birds. Now comes the question: Do parakeets form a bond with humans? I have absolutely no doubt about that, but this bond is of a different nature and quality than the bond to other parakeets. The human is a wonderful supplement for the animal, but it cannot replace the parakeet mate. What characteristics actually determine that a particular partner is chosen over many others? The story of how male and female become a pair is fascinating, and so I have dedicated an entire chapter to that topic in this book.

From Necessity to virtue

Life in a flock of parakeets is relatively peaceful. There are no hierarchies like those existing among many other animal species. A pecking order, common in a chicken yard, is also unfamiliar to these little parrots. However, small arguments do arise periodically, especially among females. The reason for that is nearly always the same: fights over food. I have been keeping parakeets in a large aviary for more than 25 years. Most of the birds are tame and friendly. I have never seen one particular bird trying to push ahead of the others to beg for my favor, a situation we know from dogs and cats. Jealousy appears to be alien to parakeets. Things heat up only when females are starting to look for nesting caves. Such a nest site, once obtained, is vigorously defended (see Intruders in the Nest Box, page 131). Apart from that, aggression does not play a major role among parakeets. There can be several reasons for that.

Necessity fosters cooperation: On one hand, parakeets do not establish territories. Instead, they move like nomads from one place to the next. On the other hand, their living conditions are harsh. In the interior of Australia, precipitation is linked to annual seasons. There may not be any rain for many months—or even for years. Thousands of these little parrots die annually in search of water. Aggression leads to injuries and diseases that will further decimate the number of birds.

Offspring to fill the ranks: The primary species-survival principle is to produce as much progeny as possible during good times, and so there is simply no time for pecking-order fights. The way nature handles this is simple. Male parakeets become sexually mature early. Their testes are already fully functional at three to four months. Such early sexual development is known only in very few bird species. Juvenile parakeets will get their adult plumage at three months, which means that—by then—the first molt will have already taken place. At such a young age, parakeets are fully capable of reproduction. Yet, nature takes this adaptation even further. In most Central European

bird species the testes become smaller outside the breeding season, and the production of sperm is terminated. The reason for this becomes intuitively obvious: It creates a weight reduction. Any parakeet owner can readily observe that all parakeets will pair off throughout the entire year. Moreover, they can do it because their testes do not lose weight and sperm production is not terminated. The surprise was indeed large when the sizes of testes were examined in wild parakeets throughout Australia. Over large areas of the interior of Australia, it is important that parakeets be able to reproduce quickly and as often as possible, in order to survive as a species. Along the coast or in areas where the living conditions are easier for parakeets, the size of their testes various just as it does in our native bird species. It appears that the reproductive pressure is less in these areas. The question remains, why exactly are our domesticated parakeets capable of breeding throughout the entire year? (see Chapter 7, New Arrivals in the Parakeet Home.)

Parakeets are particularly fond of rowanberries. They are an ideal vitamin source, especially during the winter months.

Behavior Patterns: Look Closely!

Those who know the behavior patterns of their feathered friends will understand them better. Behavior is an expression of the world of feelings, needs, and intellectual capabilities. The ability to interpret your parakeets' behavior will be the key to a better relationship between you and your parakeets. Observe your birds closely every day. If you do that, you will learn in a relatively short period to assess the condition of your little parrots correctly.

What Your Parakeets Are Trying to "Tell" You

Parakeets have a certain sound repertoire that helps them principally to organize life in a flock.

Song: The sounds given off by parakeets have little in common with melodic birdsongs. These sounds are neither rich in variety nor particularly melodic. However, for the social life of these birds they have a very large significance.

Contact call: Parakeets use this call to maintain contact with each other. It helps them locate the presence of other parakeets, even when they cannot be seen. Paired males and females have a mutual contact call. Surprisingly, it is nearly always the male that imitates the call of the female. That makes sense, because after all, scientific investigations have revealed that females are much slower in mimicking the calls of males. It seems to be in doubt, however, whether this call supports the pair bond. Essentially, it is the "adhesive" of a parakeet pair partnership.

Alarm call: This call is easy to distinguish from the contact call. The sound is short and shrill, and it is used to warn the flock that danger is approaching. Our domesticated parakeets usually make this sound when a large bird can be seen close to the window or flying above an aviary, or when some other noise frightens the birds.

Chirping: When your parakeets are chirping, their body plumage is fluffed up and the eyes are partially closed. This sound is a sign of their well-being, and it can frequently be heard at twilight.

Courtship song: During courtship, the male chirps at his intended female. This song is part of the courtship ritual (see page 118).

Screeching: These deafening sounds can be heard throughout the day. They express general excitement; unfortunately, we often do not recognize the reason for such screeching.

Clues to the Body Language of Parakeets

Preening: Only a perfectly clean plumage guarantees optimal flight performance. Consequently, the birds spend a lot of time preening every day. In contrast to large parrot species, parakeets have a fat gland, also referred to as the preen (oil) gland or uropygial gland. This fat makes the feathers pliable and water repellent. During the preening session, the little bird rubs its head at the preen gland and then distributes the fat over the feathers. With obvious relish, the bird pulls each feather through its beak. Around the anal region, where dirt can easily accumulate, the bird uses its claws to remove any debris.

For proper preening a parakeet needs to be essentially loose jointed.

Mutual preening: Also called "allo-preening" this is a type of massage among parakeets. When doing this, they nibble around the head region of the partner. This behavior serves to strengthen their bond, and is an excellent indicator of individual pairs.

Billing: Two parakeets lock their beaks at a right angle with each other. That is an expression of affection.

Threatening: A tense body posture, tightly clinging plumage, and extended neck vertebrae and head facing an opponent signals "Watch out for me." This warning is further emphasized with a threatening sound. If the opponent cannot be intimidated, the parakeet will make itself larger, open its beak, and hack at the opponent. In most cases, the opponent will fly away. Such encounters rarely ever develop into a real fight.

Sleeping: The birds sit on their perch, and have their heads bent with the beak tugged under the feathers on their backs. The plumage is generally fluffed up, and the eyes are closed. Frequently, one leg is retracted into the abdominal plumage. Could your parakeets be dreaming about an adventurous day with you? Much suggests this is so. French scientists have learned that some bird species can dream. Unfortunately, they have not yet investigated the sleep of parakeets.

Yet I am almost certain that parakeets dream. Therefore, do not wake up your parakeet too suddenly; the bird might panic. Caution! Only sick birds sleep all day.

MY PET

Getting to know your parakeets

Become a behavioral scientist and record the behavior of your birds for three days, 20 minutes each at different times of the day (twice per day) in a logbook. Record the types of behavior discussed in this book, such as preening, resting, or mutual preening.

The test starts:

Establish a checklist, where the respective behavior is listed and the duration of that behavior. For instance, if you notice preening three times during the observation period, you should make three vertical marks, and record the duration of each. It is important that you concentrate only on one particular bird. This is always the very first step for every behavioral scientist to get to know an animal.

My test results:

Wing flapping: This refers to rapid beating of wings extended while the bird is holding on to the perch or cage mesh with its feet. Young birds do this to develop their musculature. In older birds, it is a sign of lacking flight opportunities.

Having Other Parakeets Around Is Important

Our domesticated parakeets originate from the wild, green parakeets of the Australian continent. Although their appearance may have changed, their social behavior has not. They still live in flocks, and so it is predicated in their genes that they need other parakeets around them. Parakeets kept as solitary birds are less interested in the world around them and can sink into apathy. They frequently suffer from boredom, because their owners cannot be around night and day. The birds have no contact, no one to talk to in their own language. Some birds like that develop behavioral impairments. However, a singly kept parakeet can thrive when given consistent, loving attention, a balanced diet, plenty of exercise, and a lot of toys to play with and chew.

With their vocalization, parakeets stimulate each other. As we know now, the mutual chirping among parakeets has a positive effect on their hormone levels. The immune system and the birds' well-being are being enhanced.

Beyond that, what is the role of human beings for parakeets? There is no doubt that humans are important for this little bird. Similarly, there is also no doubt that a deep bond can develop between bird and human. However, the animal companion is no substitute for the complicated human relationship network. People need people, and nobody doubts that. What is surprising, however, is that animals are being denied the same basic need: Parakeets thrive with other parakeets around them. When you are selecting your birds (in a pet shop, at a breeder's, or at an animal shelter), check whether pairs have already been formed among those birds available. If so, try not to separate such pairs, but take both birds home with you if you can.

All About Compatibility

Keeping pairs: Generally, the two partners are getting along well, and to observe a pair displaying all of the typical behaviors is a lot of fun. There are no problems with offspring as long as there is no nest box (see page 116) available to the birds.
Keeping females only: I advise against that, because females often do not get along with each other and there can be a fair bit of aggression.
Keeping males only: Males are usually very compatible with each other and there are rarely any (physical) arguments; however, they miss communication with the opposite sex. Males are simply males. It is not uncommon for such males to become homosexual.

There Must Be Order: Classification of Parakeets

The Swedish scientist Carl von Linné discovered—during his numerous expeditions about 300 years ago—how important a principle of order (structural organization of species and species groups) is for the abundance of plants and animals.

Because of Linné, there are no misunderstandings among scientists throughout the world when allocating

---

Flying is the spectacular skill of parakeets. Provide as many free-flight opportunities for your birds as possible.
▾

scientific animal names. With such a system, it is obvious to all: *Melopsittacus undulatus* is the parakeet. Whether Chinese, American, or German—all of them accept this classification principle. However, this classification is *not* a system arbitrarily designed by humans. Instead it is because complicated living beings have—in the course of their evolutionary development—originated from simple organisms. Therefore, this classification is based on the natural relationships of animals. The zoological profile of the parakeet is as follows:

Class: *Aves* (Birds)
Order: *Psittaciformes* (Parrots and cockatoos)
Family: *Psittacidae* (True parrots)
Genus: *Melopsittacus* (Broadtailed parrot)
Species: *undulates* (Parakeet [with wave lines])

A flock of wild parakeets in their native Australian surroundings have finally found a watering hole.

Popular Color Varieties

There are numerous color varieties of parakeets now. They all have originated from that bird with a green and blue plumage. Those were the ancestors of our colorful flock of birds.

Bird fanciers who want to present their birds at a show must adhere to many rules and guidelines. It is not easy to become "best bird" at a show.

Beauty Contest

For instance, a parakeet must be taught how to sit in a display cage and how to behave when there. The posture of a bird on show will be included in the evaluation, as well as many other features. The British were the first to hold public shows of parakeets. Nowadays there are numerous parakeet breeder associations around the world. These organizations provide information about what breeding guidelines need to be maintained. Just as for human beauty contests, there is an international forum for parakeets. After all, one wants to know which is the most attractive bird in the world. Individual, regional associations have become affiliated with the WBO (World Budgerigar Association). In 2003, this Association established a parakeet color scheme according to Pantone. (Pantone is a standardized series of thousands of colors, each with a specific formulation and identification number. PMS colors are duplicated in swatch books and in computer-graphics programs to allow exact duplication of colors in printing and other marking processes, such as sign-making. Many stylists use Pantone color targets when designing new products.) This color scheme helps any jury categorize colors. Here are some of the characteristics that are evaluated on parakeets: Body length from top of head to tip of tail must be at least $8\frac{1}{2}$ inches (21.6 cm). Longer is permitted, but shorter is not. The head must be large, round, white, and symmetrical when viewed from every perspective. The wings must be located exactly above the rump; the tips of the wings must not be crossed over each other. The distance from the center of the chest to the outer end of the primary feathers must be 4 inches (9.5 cm). The bird must be healthy and clean, without any feathers missing. The overall picture of body form—head, mask, wing, and beak—must be harmonious. There is no question—beauty among parakeets has its price, but it remains to be seen whether the price is worth it.

TIP

Parakeet show standards

Parakeets are available in about 100 different color varieties. At bird shows, we can now see standard parakeets that are distinctly larger than normal parakeets. However, these super-specimens can have health disadvantages.

Portraits of Parakeet Breeds—at a Glance

◀ **Light-winged, yellow-faced opaline**

The wings of light-winged parakeets are allowed to have only very faint undulating marks. The first light-winged parakeets appeared in Australia in about 1930. Later on, they reached Germany via Great Britain.

Superb Specimens ▶

Left: On the left is an opaline spangle blue; on the right is a rainbow parakeet. The plumage of "rainbows" has colors that melt into each other.

▲

Cinnamon opaline dark green

The feathers of cinnamon parakeets are softer and finer than those of other parakeets.

▲

Cinnamon opaline dark green

These parakeets have brown markings instead of black ones. This phenomenon is caused by a different melanin distribution in the plumage. It can occur in all normal colors as well as in opalines.

Recessive pied ▶ yellow-faced mauve

Recessive pieds have randomly distributed body markings. Recessive pieds remain black after sexual maturity: There is no iris ring.

▲

Recessive pied yellow-faced mauve

Because of their markings, these birds are also referred to as Harlequins or Danish Pied (because of their origin).

Fallow dark blue

This is a very attractive parakeet with distinctive cheek markings. Fallow parakeets appeared as early as the 1930s among the stock of German breeders.

Dark blue

This blue variety of a "normal" parakeet has the same feather markings as the wild form.

White, dark blue ▶ and gray, yellow white

A delicate blue plumage characterizes the color variety white, dark blue. In gray, yellow parakeets, the wave markings are light gray instead of black. The base color of the rump and the abdominal region is substantially lighter than that of "normal" parakeets.

▲
Gray green
This commercially bred variety complies fully with the required standards, just like all portraits shown on these pages.

▲
Light green parakeet
The so-called "green series" among parakeets includes the colors light green, dark green, olive green, gray green, and Lutino.

Light-winged olive green ▶
The cheek patches in this variety are dark violet. This attractive male enjoys fresh, juicy leaves.

▲
Light-winged olive green
In light-winged parakeets the wings are allowed to have "washed out" wave markings only.

◀ Recessive pied olive green

In recessive pieds, the cere does not turn blue, but instead remains pink. Therefore, this cock is easy to mistake for a hen.

▲

Recessive pied olive green

This is an attractive form from among the more than 100 different color varieties of domesticated parakeets available.

▲

Opaline violet colors

This variety is characterized by very attractive, rich plumage color. In opalines, the back of the head and neck are almost (or totally) devoid of markings, and there are hardly any wavelike markings on their backs.

▲

Opaline violet colors

In this attractive head portrait, the dense plumage shows a parakeet in top physical condition.

Cinnamon light green ▶

In contrast to most other mutations, cinnamon parakeets have brown wave markings. Moreover, the cinnamon color usually brightens up the base colors.

Gray parakeet

The base color is gray with the characteristic parakeet markings. The cheek patches are gray in this mutation, and the long tail feathers are black.

▼

Cinnamon light green

The six brown throat spots are conspicuous in this photo-graph. The cere in males is blue; in females it is beige to brown.

How Parakeets Like to Live

Even as pets, parakeets can lead a very good life—
provided you take fully into account the requirements
of your feathered housemates.

A Home to Feel Comfortable in

A spacious, attractive, and functionally equipped home is the dream of every human. Parakeets want the same thing, and it is usually not difficult to meet the desires of your feathered friends.

Without question, the most important thing for these little Australian parrots is the company of their own kind. That applies to their life in the wild as well as when they are kept as pets. Yet, a spacious cage and the daily free flight with discovery expeditions through your home also contribute significantly to their well-being.

Lots of Room in a Comfortable Parakeet Home

Your parakeets' feeling of well-being depends of course on many things, such as having other parakeets around, a healthy diet, and hygienic conditions. However, cage size and furnishings are also of importance for the parakeet home. These little parrots will make it quite clear to us by their behavior whether they like their home or not. Their protest against a cage that is far too small is not expressed by means of loud screeching, but instead mainly by a display of apathy. They are sitting on their perch in total boredom, hardly making a sound. Many people believe that small birds require only small cages. However, such an assumption is—as you can imagine—very wrong!

Macaws and African gray parrots, the large cousins of parakeets, fly much less than these little powerhouses from the Australian continent. Yet this does not mean that we can accommodate large parrots in small cages. They too require a lot of room!

When the cage fulfills parakeets' certain basic requirements, an important cornerstone for their well-being has been laid. Fortunately, there are now reliable and practical recommendations for the correct home for birds that have been scientifically tested and thoroughly tried in practice. What is important, though, is to select the correct one.

This is a lot of ▶
fun: A parakeet
takes advantage
of the indoor
fountain made of
lava rock for
drinking and
splashing.

The Right Place for the Parakeet Home

Parakeets are sociable birds, and therefore their cage can indeed be in the center of family activities. They enjoy the talking and gossiping of people around them; maybe it reminds them of their own twittering. However, the kitchen is the wrong location. There, these little birds—whether in a cage or during indoor free-flight sessions—are exposed to many dangers, such as hot stove burners, food odors, pots with hot contents, pivot-hung windows, empty containers to slide into, and open cupboard doors. In short, anyone who keeps parakeets in the kitchen must be extremely watchful so that nothing happens to them.

In any event, it is better to keep the cage in the living room, where the family gets together and where there may be natural sunlight. Sunlight contains ultraviolet rays, which are essential for bone structure. The importance of well-lit rooms for the well-being of the small parrots has been demonstrated in an impressive manner by Sandra Zipp of the University of Bern in Switzerland in her doctoral dissertation. She gave parakeets a choice between brightly illuminated and dark rooms. The result was unequivocal: The parakeets decided on the brightly lit room. Not as clear-cut was their response to neon light that flickered with variable frequency (100 Hz and 42 kHz). In contrast to the parakeet eye, our own eye cannot perceive this flickering. Our little parrots do not seem to be affected by neon light. The fear expressed by many readers, that neon light is not good for the birds, seems to be groundless.

Elevated location: The birdcage should not be placed on the floor, but at eye level with adults, on a cupboard or cabinet that is not too high, or on a shelf or a dedicated stand for birdcages, as a permanent location. Parakeets in nature prefer highly elevated rest and sleeping places as protection against enemies. They are afraid when they are too close to the ground. Ideally, you should place the cage in a well-lit corner, from where the birds have a good overview of their surroundings and the activities in the room. The windowsill is not an ideal place. It is generally too low, too cold in the winter, and too hot in the summer. Moreover, during the summer there is a significant danger of heatstroke.

◀ *Soft landing. Golliwoog (Creeping Inch plant, Callisia repens) is a food plant that is commercially available in pet shops. Many parakeets get excited about this tasty green feed.*

Free of vibrations: The location for the parakeet cage must also be vibration-free. In any case, that eliminates the refrigerator, washing machine, and dishwasher.

Draft-free: Drafty air circulation is pure venom for parakeets. Although these birds endure large temperature variations, they are very sensitive to drafty conditions. Using the flame of a candle, you can check for this. The flame will flicker even before we notice there is a draft.

Other pets: The cage must always be out of reach of other pets in the home. Birds are on the menu of predators, such as cats. Therefore, your parakeets are always in danger from the velvet-pawed hunter. I would not guarantee the behavior of ANY cat, in terms of a reaction to parakeets. Maybe someday the feline's hunting instinct will take over, and she will pounce . . . if given the opportunity. I have seen how both animals can live peacefully in the same room, yet I still advise against it on principle. And how about dogs? Well-trained dogs, especially those breeds with a strong guarding instinct, are generally not as dangerous for parakeets as cats are. Still, the cage must not be within reach of a dog; otherwise the little parrots will be severely stressed and frightened.

Changing cage location: Experienced parakeet breeders may well shake their heads at the suggestion that once the bird has settled in, you can change the location of the cage occasionally within the same room. However, it allows the birds to get a different perspective on the room. An occasional change of perspective is not only exciting but also stimulating.

CHECKLIST

Free-flight Dangers

When parakeets are flying freely in your home, you must eliminate some danger sources.

- ○ Secure open windows with screens.

- ○ Cover large windowpanes with curtains or retractable shades.

- ○ Turn off and cover cooking tops.

- ○ Do not leave pointed and sharp objects in the room where the birds are flying.

- ○ Do not leave tall containers with water standing around.

- ○ All slots and crevices, e.g., behind bookshelves, should be sealed off or suitably enlarged.

- ○ Relocate electric power cables behind boards.

- ○ Make sure there is no bird sitting on top of a door or in a drawer that you want to close.

- ○ Remove alcohol, pencils, plant fertilizer, cleaning agents, and strong spices.

- ○ When birds have access to the bathroom, make sure the toilet lid is closed.

- ○ Do not use insect spray in a room where there are birds.

In nature, all animals are exposed to diverse environmental stimuli. How different, and especially how boring, must the world seem to those animals, such as birds, that live exclusively indoors. It can only be good for the psyche of birds if they can see their indoor world occasionally from a different perspective. Boredom is venom for the psyche of all pets, and parakeets are no exception. They need a lot of change.

The Basic Home

The bigger the cage, the better, is the maxim. For parakeets, the largest possible cage is just right. Yet, no cage can ever be sufficiently large to fully satisfy the innate flight requirements of these birds; therefore, a daily free flight indoors or in an aviary is an absolute must. Such a free flight is even more important when the birds live in a small cage.

This is what an attractive bird home for two parakeets could look like. ▼

Cage sizes: The minimum measurements for a parakeet home for two birds should be 28 inches (70 cm) length, 16 inches (40 cm) width, and 20 inches (50 cm) height. My recommendation: While you are at it, take the larger one with 39 inches (1 m) length, 20 inches (50 cm) width, and 32 inches (80 cm) height. Cages with a fold-up mesh roof, where a perch can be fitted, are ideal. This facilitates an easy, stress-free exit for the birds from the cage. During their exploratory excursions, the birds will automatically climb onto this perch above you to look out into the room without their views being obstructed by a wire screen. This generates self-confidence and encourages free flight in the room.

Cage wire: Parakeets like cages with horizontal bars instead of vertical bars, where they can climb up the sides of cage more easily. Therefore, the cage should have at least two sides with horizontal bars. The wire bars of this bird home should be made of chrome or brass. Plastic-coated wire cannot withstand parakeet beaks for very long. Make sure that the distance between adjacent parallel bars is not greater than $1/2$ inch (12 mm), because these clever little parrots can force their way through the bars without much effort, in order to get out of the cage.

Cage door: It is very important how the cage door opens. It should open out and down 90 degrees to a level horizontal position. This way it works as an ideal departure and landing ramp during the free-flying session. It is also advisable to have a second door in the cage roof, provided you do not have a cage with a removable roof. A second door is useful for routine maintenance work in the cage.

Bottom tray: Commercially available cages have a bottom tray made of plastic and easy to clean. This is extremely important for the hygiene inside the bird home (see page 83).

Note: I categorically reject cages with a bottom wire mesh, because it prevents the birds from happily foraging along the cage floor, a habit that is innate to their nature. This picking along the ground is an essential component in the behavior repertoire of parakeets. Moreover, feces become stuck in the bottom

available cages, they are usually made of plastic or compressed cardboard. Replace some of them with natural branches. Branches from untreated fruit, birch, and elder trees are suitable for that. **Important:** Perches should be of such a diameter that the birds' claws rarely ever touch each other when gripping around a branch. Natural branches have a significant advantage: The birds love to chew on

DID YOU KNOW THAT . . .

. . . birds can fly very fast?

In nature, parakeets can reach flight speeds of up to 75 mph (120 km/h). Most economical—in terms of energy consumption—are long, straight flights with an average speed of 26 mph (42 km/h). If the birds are forced to change altitude because of adverse wind conditions, that is, if they have to fly up and down in a wavelike pattern, the flight speed is approximately 17 mph (27 km/h). Parakeets acquire their energy principally through fat metabolism.

wire mesh, which makes cage cleaning more difficult.

Functional Cage Furnishings

When it comes to furnishing a home, humans are guided by their personal taste. I do not know whether animals have an aesthetic perception, but I do not believe that they do. Therefore, because we do not know any better, the furnishings of a parakeet cage are best in line with biological considerations.

Perches: Perches are part of the basic furnishings of a new cage. In commercially

them, and if they are of different diameter, the birds are forced to continuously adjust the grip of their feet around them. This then protects the underside of the feet against pressure sores (often followed by very painful inflammations). Another important advantage of natural branches is that the length of the claws is kept in check by natural means, and the stressful claw trimming procedure—for you as the parakeet owner—is usually completely avoided.

Apart from that, the musculature of legs and feet of the birds is being exercised.

Cage liners: Special papers can be used to line the bottom of the cage and are readily available. You can also use newspaper, paper towels, or butcher paper. Cob bedding or other loose bird "litter" is also available but can rapidly become moldy or smelly.

Food and water containers: Cage size permitting, you should offer your birds a food dispenser as well as a ceramic food dish, available from pet shops. This sounds somewhat superfluous, but it is a distinct benefit for the birds. A shallow dish has the advantage of the bird being able to select from among individual grain types. Parakeets seem to prefer particular grains on certain days. Just like humans, birds have particular requirements at different times. Moreover, seeds do not become buried under empty seed husks in a food bowl. The seed dispenser is more often a safety backup, so that there is always sufficient clean seed available, and it supplies the birds for one or two days if you should happen to be away. Pet shops offer suitable water dispensers made of plastic that can be attached to the outside of the cage, with the opening protruding into the cage. **Caution:** Some birds require a long time to learn how to drink from a water dispenser. Until that time, it is advisable to place an additional water bowl, made of earthenware or ceramic, in the cage. Once the bird knows how to drink from a water dispenser, you can remove the bowl.

Beak-grinding stone or cuttlebone: The stone supplies the bird with calcium and at the same time also serves as a grinding stone for the beak. This extra calcium supplement is important for mature female parakeets.

Birdbath: Although it may not rain for many months in parakeets' native country, all parakeets love to splash around in their own "bathtub." Therefore, a little "bathhouse" is quite appropriate in a parakeet cage. It is advisable to buy a covered bathhouse made of plastic, which is fitted tightly into the open cage door space. Make sure the bottom of the bath is grooved so that the birds can move about without slipping. The easiest way to accustom a parakeet to a new bathtub is by placing wet leaves (spinach, dandelion, or lettuce) into the birdbath. A parakeet will slide through these leaves and get its plumage wet. Later on, put some lukewarm water—to a depth of a few inches—into the bathtub. Instead of a regular birdbath, you can also use a flowerpot saucer made of earthenware or ceramic.

The Importance of Play

Physical activity is important. However, that does not mean that the cage must be overloaded with toys. Less is often more, provided it is the right toy. Parakeets like to play. You can promote this drive for playing with relative ease. Branches and twigs are the most cost-effective toys, and birds like them. Moreover, such natural toys have the advantage that you can easily and cheaply replace them once they are severely damaged by the chewing activities of the birds. Every replacement represents a new attraction for the birds. Parakeets like to use a swing, and so I recommend you place two swings made of wood inside the cage. It is better to have two than just one, in order to avoid arguments between the birds.

Basic Cage Furnishings—
at a Glance

Food bowl and drink ▶ dispenser

A food bowl and a drink dispenser are for parakeets the natural way to feed and drink water. Both are useful only when they have been thoroughly cleaned.

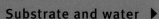

◀ Beak-grinding stone (cuttlebone)

A beak-grinding stone and fresh food provide for the bodily well-being of your parakeets. Offer fresh food in a dedicated bowl or as a component of an activity program.

Substrate and water ▶

Substrate on the cage bottom is important for hygienic reasons. Among other things, it binds liquid (urine) and feces. A parakeet must be provided with fresh water daily.

Small wooden ladders and plastic balls with bells inside are also recommended activity objects. Pet shops now have entertaining toys available especially for birds that can be combined with twigs and branches in the free-flight room. Playgrounds outside the cage are also popular. These are a type of carrying tray, to which one can quickly attach a perch, a ladder, and a wooden hoop. These "adventure playgrounds" are available commercially in various models. They can be placed anywhere in a room, or can even be attached on top of the cage roof.

Note: Keep changing the toys, which means placing a particular toy into the cage for one to two weeks and then replacing it with another toy. If old toys are left in the cage for prolonged periods, they become boring for the birds, but with frequent changes, the toys remain interesting to them.

A bird that has access to a hanging play gym will not be a nuisance while flying freely in a room. The feces always drops into a drip tray (not shown) that is attached to these gyms.

Exercise Is Always Good

Parakeets are excellent flyers. What could be better for them than to have you actively support their aerial acrobatics? One possibility is a large outdoor aviary, but even a daily free flight indoors already enhances their quality of life.

WHEN, AFTER considerable thought, you have decided to keep a small flock of parakeets, I advise you to build an aviary outdoors. Before building an outside aviary, check the construction regulations from the proper authorities, such as the local building and zoning department. Also, find out if the neighbors will mind having an aviary next door. You also need to be clear in your mind about a few points.

Please, Keep in Mind!

Keeping parakeets outdoors for the entire year involves considerable work and a few things that need to be considered up front.

Space: An aviary requires a lot of space, because it has to be sufficiently large for the parakeets to actually fly in it. After all, the parakeets do not have their daily free flight indoors (see page 46). Yet, such a large outdoor aviary is an absolute winner for parakeets. The birds will be able to move about extensively all day and engage in their normal social behavior to the fullest.

Note: An aviary deserves that name only if it enables the birds to practice their innate flight behavior. Most aviaries, especially the portable indoor aviaries available from pet shops, are too small for keeping parakeets properly outdoors. Moreover, they do not provide adequate free-flight space. Of course, these large cages provide excellent accommodation for parakeets that are kept indoors, as well as for temporary, hourly periods outdoors. Make sure, however, if you are using such a mobile cage for limited time outdoors, never to leave it in direct sun or in drafty conditions.

Location: A partially sunny and semi-shaded location is ideal for an aviary. If this is not possible, use a sunny location. Parakeets love warmth and brightness. If the temperature is too high, it is easy to provide suitable shade, with fine-meshed nets available from pet shops or plant nurseries. Cheaper solutions are also possible. Moreover, the birds must be protected against draft air and strong winds. My advice: Attach a transparent plastic sheet to the side of the aviary that is exposed to inclement weather conditions.

Temperature: The aviary must be constructed in such a way that the temperature inside never drops below 43°F (6°C). Higher temperatures are better for the well-being of parakeets. My studies have shown that these birds are the most active at a temperature range from 54 to 86°F (12 to 30°C). They bill frequently, fly about, and investigate new objects. At low temperatures they sit on a perch with their plumage fluffed up.

◀ *This is an aviary at a wind-protected site. It offers sufficient room and diversity for a small flock of parakeets.*

In that position, heat loss is minimal. Air becomes trapped within the fluffed-up feathers, which has an insulating effect. When it is hot out, the parakeets sit on a perch with extended wings and are panting through an open beak.

Training: It is far more difficult to train a number of birds together than just two of them, because the birds are seeking contact with each other and not the proximity of humans. However, with some patience and sensitivity it is possible to hand-tame some birds. About half of my 28 birds are tame.

Maintenance: A small flock of birds produces more dirt than just two birds. It goes without saying, then, that the maintenance efforts are also higher for an aviary.

The Outdoor Aviary

For a maximum of 10 parakeets, the aviary should be at least 10 feet (3 m) long, 5 feet (1.5 m) high, and 39 inches (1 m) wide. With a bit of luck, you can probably find a large off-the-shelf aviary in pet shops or on the Internet. Many pet shops are able to give you sound professional advice and will order a custom-made aviary for you from a specialty manufacturer. Anybody with some repairperson skills and sufficient confidence can, of course, build his or her own aviary.

Brand "home made": My aviary has been custom-made, according to my preferences and requirements. It is 20 feet (6 m) long, 13 feet (4 m) high, and 8 feet (2.5 m) wide, and is located along a protected side of the house. The roof of the house forms the aviary roof. The frame consists of aluminum bracing of 2 × 2 inches (5 × 5 cm) thickness, which is screwed together. Aluminum frames have the advantage of being stable, weather-resistant, and easy to clean.

The wire mesh is attached to the inside of the frame ($\frac{3}{4} \times \frac{3}{4}$ mesh size [2 × 2 cm]), so that on the outside a type of window or door frame is formed. Three sides of the aviary consist of wire netting. The entrance door is also formed by an aluminum frame, with a transparent plastic panel screwed against the inside of the frame. So that the birds cannot escape when the door is opened, a curtain made of bast (natural wooden fibers) cords is attached to the door frame.

The floor of the aviary is laid out with concrete tiles, fitted closely against the aluminum frame so that neither rats nor other vermin can get into the aviary. A layer of bird sand covers the concrete tiles to a thickness of about ½ inch (1 cm). In the winter, I seal the frame structure as follows: I nail ¼ inch (.5 cm) thick plastic sheeting against the inside and outside of the wooden frames, which fit tightly against the aviary frame. This way an airspace is being created that has a heat insulating effect. The wood is painted with a non-toxic, environmentally friendly lacquer. These wooden frames are then fitted into the aluminum frame, where they are attached with clips, and the "windows" for the aviary are ready. They have the advantage that on good weather days they can be removed easily. On very cold days, I heat the aviary with a small electric oil heater that is controlled by a thermostat. The temperature in the aviary never drops below 43°F (6°C). I am sure that there are better heating systems around, but since I live in a temperate climate, this type of heating is sufficient. This type of construction has proven to be effective; however, there are, no doubt, others that can also be used.

Note: The instructions given here are meant only as a suggestion in order to provide ideas. Whatever the type of construction an aviary is, it must provide heated and protected accommodation for the well-being of the bird flock through all seasons of the year. There are also many suggestions on the Internet for the construction of bird aviaries.

▶ **1** **Smart bird.** How to reach the millet if it is suspended by a string? Very simple: You just pull up the entire seed spike and the food is at hand.

▶ **2** **Get rid of the lid.** With the aid of its beak, the parakeet pushes the lid aside and helps itself to the seeds. Parakeets are very intelligent birds.

Aviary Furnishings

The required layout for an aviary conforms essentially to that of a traditional cage. Food and drinking bowls must be positioned so that neither feces nor other dirt can fall into these containers. I feed and water my birds on top of an 8-inch (20-cm) wide, 39-inch (1-m) long board. The board is attached at a height of 5 feet (1.5 m), resting on angle braces, which have been attached by means of screws to the aluminum frame. Consequently, cleaning this board is very easy. I only have to remove it and rinse it off with water. The location of the board has been selected so that the birds cannot soil it. I have two perches firmly attached in front of the board. They are fixed-point and permanent landing sites, respectively. These permanently attached perches provide the birds with a degree of security.

Landing site and nibbling material: There are "trees" in my aviary. For that, I look for thick branches (up to 8 feet [2.5 m] tall) as well as for twigs with leaves. Usually I position them vertically—sort of like a tree in the landscape—in the aviary, and secure them with wire or rope against the wire sides. The branches are placed in a water bucket, which is covered by a fine mesh grid so that birds cannot fall into the bucket and drown. The water keeps the branches fresh for quite a while, and the parakeets enjoy them very much. The branches are allowed to wobble and move, very much like trees in nature. The birds really enjoy landing on these swinging branches. The enjoyment becomes even more intense when branches and twigs are brought in soaking wet. It is sheer pleasure to see the birds virtually "bathing" among the wet leaves. Nontoxic branches and twigs are from oak, alder, elder, chestnut, lime, poplar, willow and fruit trees. I know these tree species will not hurt the parakeets; however, with other types of branches I suggest caution, especially with yew trees. All branches are replaced every four to five weeks.

Toys: Exploring new things keeps the birds mentally fit. Even the entire flock occasionally gets new toys (see pages 40, 104), but as mentioned earlier, in this case, less is more. Do not obstruct the aviary, and keep in mind that the birds need sufficient flying space.

Parakeets Must Fly

Anyone who keeps his parakeet all day in a little cage without offering some free-flight time can be assured that in due course the birds will display behavioral disorders. In a particular study, Swiss biologist Kurt Banzer was able to show that birds that were not given some free-flying time would eventually hardly ever fly when the cage door was opened for them. Instead, they remained on their perches and continuously flapped their wings. This behav-

---

TIP

A room for birds in your home

If you can provide a dedicated bird room for a small flock of parakeets, you must make sure that there is adequate ventilation. Because of their high metabolic rate, parakeets need a lot of oxygen. For bird keepers, a dusty bird room is often the source of allergies; therefore, caution is advised!

"I was here first." *Minor disagreements are common among parakeets.*

ioral disorder is referred to as "winging." In addition to that, there can also be weight and respiratory problems.

To demonstrate how parakeets can suffer when they are not permitted to fly, just imagine the following scenario: You have spent your entire life exclusively in a small room. You are being given food and water and occasionally a friendly word. There is adequate and loving care in terms of food and social contact, but would you be contented with such a situation? Probably not. On one hand, your curiosity would not be satisfied, and on the other hand, your physical fitness would suffer under such an existence. A parakeet reacts similarly, and the proverbial saying about "life in a gilded cage" is very appropriate here. At this point, I do not want to give specific time requirements for how long your parakeets should be able to fly

freely every day. Instead, provide this pleasure for your birds as often as you possibly can.

Before you permit your birds the first free-flying laps indoors, you should always remember these precautions:
▶ Close all doors and windows; be particularly cautious with pivot-hung windows: There is a great risk of injuries, and the birds can escape.
▶ Make large windowpanes visible for the birds, or pull the curtains shut.

Of course, there are still other danger sources for free flying birds in your home. I have summarized these in a checklist on page 37.

For young birds these first flying hours are very exciting. Do not worry, parakeets are very smart and learn quickly, and soon you will be able to enjoy every minute of their aerial exploits. The more comfortable and secure a parakeet becomes, the more boldly it will attempt to satisfy its curiosity and nibbling instinct. Nothing is safe from its beak, and most certainly, some magazines or maybe even a book will become a shredded victim. However, there is a solution to this problem. You can channel the curiosity and the chewing instinct of your parakeets. For instance, you can build your pets a climbing tree or an exciting landing site that is attached to the ceiling of the room. Generally, the birds prefer natural branches to your furniture.

The Climbing Tree

An indoor climbing tree has large advantages not only for parakeets, but also for you, the owner. For the birds, such a tree is a place of security. Here they can chew and climb to their hearts' content. The furniture and other inventory of your home will be spared unsightly gnawing marks, and bird droppings will not land on the kitchen or living room floor. As is often the case, the most useful things are easy to build. **Assembly instructions:** Get yourself a (heavy) container, about 20 inches (50 cm) high (made of earthenware or ceramic), with a diameter of about 32 inches (80 cm). Place some thick

MY PET

What are your parakeets' favorite toys?

Parakeets are born individualists. Every one of them has a distinct preference for certain games. One may like using the swing, the other prefers to push little balls around, and the next one likes to be a "bell ringer."

Start of the test:

First, find out when the birds are in the mood to play. Then give them a choice of different toys, for instance a grape floating in a shallow bowl of water, a lattice ball, or uncooked noodles. Record which toy the bird is starting to play with and for how long. Repeat these trials several times.

My test results:

▲

Fresh food served differently: From a wicker table it tastes even better.

branches vertically into the container, and secure them with heavy rocks. The container is then filled with potting soil. To make the structure more stable, you should connect the main branches with cross branches, which can be secured with cord and natural fiber threads. Make sure that the cross branches do not protrude beyond the edge of the container, so that bird droppings actually fall onto the potting soil below. For such a climbing tree, you can use branches from a nearby forest or out of your yard. In this case, you can be assured that the branches are free of pollutants and insecticides. You should periodically replace the branches with fresh ones. This enhances the birds' curiosity and increases their gnawing fun.

Location: Place the climbing tree as far away as possible from the cage, so that your birds have to fly back and forth when they want to eat or drink. That keeps them fit. The ideal location is in the proximity of a window, because there is a lot of light. It is also advisable to build a second climbing tree. You leave one tree permanently at one location and move the second tree around. The birds will fly a lot more, because this way you can readily adjust their flight paths by increasing distances and routes. That makes parakeets curious. I have observed this in birds at a friend's place. The effect was impressive. The birds are just as alert and agile as birds kept in a large aviary. However, there is also a "win" here for the owner. The parakeets are even less interested in your home furniture—I did not see any beak marks on my friend's furniture.

Welcome Home

The decision has been made: Two or more parakeets will become the new family members. Now it is important to make sure that the birds build trust in you right from the start.

Purchase and Selection of Parakeets

When you see these cute birds in the display cage of a pet shop, as they are affectionately chirping to and cuddling with each other, you may want to buy the entire lot! Yet, caution must prevail; such spontaneous purchases can easily bring severe disappointments. You will need to properly prepare for such a purchase.

Parakeets enter into a bond with humans as well as with other parakeets. They will suffer when there is a constant change in human partners. Therefore, you will need to consider fully whether you and your children are ready to accept the responsibility for at least two birds for the next 10 to 15 years; that is how old pet parakeets can get.

Where Do You Find Your Feathered Friends?

There are essentially four possibilities where you can get the parakeets of your dreams: at a breeder, at a pet shop, from an animal shelter, or from private hands.

Responsible Breeders

Blind trust may be adequate, but direct control is better. That is particularly true when purchasing an animal. The personal acquaintance with a breeder is a duty. My experiences in that respect have been mostly positive. The majority of breeders handle birds lovingly and professionally. However, just like every-

where else, there are also black sheep. Therefore, I am offering a few tips: Ask yourself whether the breeder keeps parakeets because of the money or because he or she genuinely enjoys them. How can you tell whether he or she is sincere? The language reveals more than one would initially expect. If he or she talks in a demeaning manner about the birds and refers to them as merchandise, or simply as "things," it is best not to pursue a sale with him or her. If the suspicion is further enhanced by dirty cages that are also too small, it

Toys for climbing ▶
or using as a swing, such as this little rope ladder, are very much enjoyed by parakeets.

Healthy Parakeets

Using just a few characteristics, even a nonprofessional can recognize whether a parakeet is healthy or not:

○ The parakeet is bright, grooms itself, and has contact with the other birds in the cage.

○ The plumage is clean, smooth, and shiny. Tail or wing feathers must not be absent.

○ The sternum (chest) of the bird must be rounded toward the outside, and must not have a sunken-in appearance.

○ The eyes are shiny and clean and do not give off any discharge.

○ The nostrils are clean, without excretions.

○ The beak is smooth and well formed.

○ The cere is clean, without signs of discharge or encrustation.

○ Feet and toes are straight and clean. The horny scales on the legs must be smooth. Two toes are pointing forward and two are pointing back.

○ The cloaca (anal region) is clean and not reddened.

○ The droppings contain a delineated white salt component of uric acid, green feces, and watery urine.

places another question mark over the quality of the birds. In a general conversation, you can easily determine whether he or she has any zoological knowledge about the birds. A good breeder knows exactly the time of the hatching of the chicks and can relate interesting details about the birds' parents and their progeny. All that would demonstrate his or her interest in the personality of the birds. Yet, even more about his or her compassion (or lack of it) for animals is being revealed by the questions to you, which should reflect the feeling of responsibility. The breeder should want to give the birds only to responsible, animal-loving people.

At the Pet Shop

Wherever you purchase a parakeet, whether it is from a breeder or in a pet shop, always cast a critical glance at the accommodation of the birds. Are the birds being kept in sufficiently large cages? Do they live in small flocks? Do they have sufficient food and fresh drinking water available? Is the cage bottom covered with clean substrate, and are there beak-grinding stones or cuttlebones or branches to gnaw on? Ask the salesperson where the birds came from. Ideally, the birds should not have traveled too far, so that they have not been exposed to too much stress. Unfortunately, long transports often lead to trauma for the birds, from which they usually recover only very slowly. In some instances, such birds will never become tame. Make sure that you do not get genetically inbred birds. Ask the dealer whether the birds are related to each other. The purpose of that question is to find out whether it is a breeder who mass-produces these birds. That is not necessarily bad, but I would always prefer parakeets to come from smaller breeding facilities.

Observe the bird(s) of your choice for a while and from a distance, and study the behavior. Is the bird active or does it sit listless in a corner? Is the bird busy and active with an object or with its siblings? Does it feed, drink and groom itself? A quiet, sleepy bird could be (but is not necessarily) sick. It could be that the bird is just having a rest. You should have a second look at that bird after some time or maybe even the next day.

Check Out an Animal Shelter

You will be doing a good deed when you take in an orphaned parakeet from an animal shelter. However, often there is a problem with this: Generally, the prior history of such birds is unknown. Behavior problems are not uncommon, especially with birds that have had different owners. Therefore, it is particularly important to take your time when selecting parakeets from such a facility. Observe the selected bird—or birds—very carefully. Make sure the bird is not pulling out its feathers. If you do not notice anything in particular and the birds are tame, you can unhesitatingly take them.

Parakeets from Friends

If you have the opportunity to acquire parakeet progeny from friends, you should not hesitate for too long. This situation is ideal. You know the owner and his or her attitude toward the birds. You can also easily check the maintenance conditions, and observe the birds at length and in peace. The birds will also profit from such an arrangement.

Carpet fringes fascinate these little parrots.

Their owner changes only once and a lot of unnecessary stress is avoided. Also, according to the U.S. Fish and Wildlife Service, no permits are required to breed parakeets. However, if in doubt, hobbyists could contact their state U.S. Fish and Wildlife Services field offices.

Leg band: Upon hatching, all juvenile parakeets should to be banded. Leg bands are not required by law, but are important for show stock, locating lost birds, and prevention of disease. Embossed in the leg band is a combination of numbers and letters that quickly reveals the origin of the bird. This way you can also make sure that parrot disease (*Psittacosis*) is not being spread (see page 91). Fortunately, this disease occurs only very rarely these days.

Not Interested in Parakeets

Our two parakeets, named Paul and Paula, have been with us for only half a year, but our 12-year-old daughter has already lost interest in looking after the birds. I would prefer to surrender the parakeets to an animal shelter.

First, try to spare your birds such a fate if they have become adjusted to you. Instead, try to reawaken your daughter's interest in the birds. Nowadays, 12-year-olds often have a full appointment calendar. During their spare time, they meet with friends or pursue a hobby intensively. In view of the weekly cage cleaning and the daily feeding and watering of the parakeets, the initial euphoria often quickly evaporates.

This is how you can reawaken interest

Appeal to your daughter's compassion. Tell her how the birds would suffer if they were torn from their familiar surroundings. Try to enhance your daughter's imagination with descriptive comparisons, for instance by suggesting how she would feel if she was taken out of her home. Tell your daughter something exciting about the life of the parakeets, for instance how colorful the world appears to them, or that the parakeet pair remains together for their entire lives. The tests that you will find in every chapter of this guide are intended to provide better and more understanding of parakeets. Try them out together with your daughter. Speak to her biology teacher, and suggest including "pet days" in the curriculum, where the children are allowed to talk about their animals. Maybe you can even let your daughter exchange information about parakeets with other parakeet owners via the Internet. There are many commendable forums.

Make a plan

In my experience, it is helpful to formulate a precise care plan for the parakeets together with your child. Such a plan should contain all daily and weekly tasks and who has to do what and when. However, it is important to monitor the compliance with such a plan, so that the birds are actually doing well. Check with your daughter that all her chores are done to your satisfaction; if they are, you should not be spare with praise. Now the child can be proud of herself. It promotes self-confidence and maybe her long-term interest in the birds. Only after these suggestions have failed should you consider a good home elsewhere for Paul and Paula.

Age at the Time of Purchase

You should buy parakeets at an age of five to six weeks. That is the best age in order to tame these birds. However, it is only a rule of thumb. I have also had good experiences with older birds when they have been kept under proper conditions. For beginners, young birds are more suitable. Nestling parakeets can be recognized as follows: The eyes—relative to the head—are very large and uniformly dark without a light-colored ring around the iris.

Distinguishing the Sexes

Upon completion of the juvenile molt (first change of feathers), the cere, the nostril area above the beak, changes color. In cocks, it becomes blue, but in hens, it is brownish beige. However, in juvenile birds, males have a pinkish cere; the females have a light blue one with white rings around the nostrils.

My Personal View About Your Purchase Choice

The "breeder ego" in humans often has no limits. Dog and cat breeds with extremely shortened muzzles have respiratory and cardiac problems; guinea pigs with hair that is too long suffer heat stress and corneal infections. There are also excessively large and heavy parakeets. The concept *torture breed* is appropriate for such breeding excesses. Most such overbred animals are not as robust and have reduced longevities. I am not necessarily an opponent of pedigree breeding, provided the well-being of the animal is the principal objective. Whether you decide on a pedigree bird is a matter of taste. However, I reject excessively heavy and overly large parakeets. As a rule, the "normal" ones are the more skilled, aerial acrobats; they are more active and live longer. My 30 years' experience concurs with relevant scientific findings.

Children and parakeets can indeed fit together. However, children must be properly instructed on the correct handling of the bird. ▶

Settling in ... Gently

Parakeets react sensitively to any change in the environment. A change from a familiar cage to a new home and the loss of a partner are severely stressful for them. You will need to make this change as easy as possible for the birds.

It is difficult to believe, yet it is true: your behavior toward the bird(s) during the first few hours of being together in the new home is decisive for the future relationship between you and your parakeets. Therefore, I recommend that you read this chapter very carefully and take its suggestions to heart.

Your Empathy Is Needed

It is hard for us to imagine the difficulties our parakeets have in adapting to a completely new world when they arrive at our home. It is always difficult to put yourself in someone else's position. Even we humans have problems with that, and even more so when it comes to animals. However, with some thoughtful consideration it is easier to understand. For the small, defenseless bird everything—and I mean everything—is very new. There are strange sounds, strange people, strange surroundings, and possibly also the separation from the other parakeets in the flock. Who would not be scared under such conditions? Imagine an orphan that is taken into a new home. The child is starting to get a foothold—initial, hesitant friendships are being formed. Suddenly the child is taken to caring foster parents. The

reaction of most children in response to such change is unambiguous: They will cry and be sad, although the foster parents are doing everything to make sure the child is content.

What does this story have to do with our small parrots? Of course, a parakeet is not a human, and its feelings are presumably not as deep. Nevertheless, the bird too perceives loneliness and fear. It has been abruptly removed from the flock at the pet shop or at the breeders, and placed into a dark box. That is a traumatic event for the small bird. Although a well-furnished cage is awaiting the parakeet, it needs time to adjust to it. At that very point, your empathy is called for.

Proceed with patience and consideration, so that your parakeet gains trust in you. The time that you are investing now will pay off later. A bird that is hand tamed will not only give you more joy but also create less work for you. For instance, it is extremely stressful for person and animal to return an untamed bird to the cage. Your feathered friends should be able to explore and experience their surroundings without haste. The birds set the pace of the adjustment process. Of course, that does not mean that you have nothing to do during that time. All you need to do is

Parakeets are superb flyers, and therefore must have some free-flight time in your home every day.

NOT put any pressure on your parakeets at that point.

Transporting Your Birds Home . . . Gently

In pet shops the birds are usually transferred into a cardboard box with a few ventilating slots. Initially there is a lot of screeching and excited running around inside the box. However, the darkness of the box screens against any fear-triggering environmental stimuli, and after a few minutes the birds have adjusted to the box. Under no conditions should you place the cardboard box into an airtight plastic bag, because the birds could suffocate in there. A basket or a cloth bag is better, but here too air must be able to enter through ventilating slots in the box. After purchasing the birds, you should drive straight home.

Once there, you have to act cautiously and skillfully: Hold the transport box against the open cage door so that the birds can change over effortlessly. With a shy bird that refuses to move, gently raise one end of the box until the occupant slides into the cage. With gentle clicking sounds and a soft voice try to establish contact with the birds. This will give the little parrots a feeling of security. Then leave the parakeets completely alone so that they can inspect their new surroundings. As soon as the birds eat and drink, the first hurdle of adjusting to the new home has been successfully overcome.

Note: Private breeders sometimes do not have a suitable box. In that case,

Building Confidence

▶ **1** **Establishing contact.** At first, the cage remains closed. The bird feels secure in there. Talk to him with a gentle, soft voice.

▶ **2** **Curiosity wins.** A piece of millet tempts the bird to nibble. Wait until the bird accepts the offer and approaches you.

▶ **3** **Tender bonds.** The first hurdle has been overcome. The bird sits confidently on your hand and enjoys feeding on the millet.

transport the birds in a cage. Remove all furnishings except for a single perch. Drape a lightweight material that is not airtight over the cage. Once at home, you simply remove the cover and then furnish the birds' home with lots of empathy.

The Parakeets in Their New Home

The first few hours are generally not very exciting. Usually the birds will sit quietly on a perch observing the surroundings and listening to the strange new noises. Gradually they will become more curious and climb in the cage. Then, cautiously and almost delicately, the wire bars and perches are nibbled on. That is the right point at which to initiate contact with your feathered housemates. Talk to them calmly and keep repeating their names. This way the birds will learn to recognize your appearance and your voice. After two or three days, they will trust you and no

longer be afraid. Some birds—and in my experience only very few—will fearfully retreat into a corner along the cage bottom or turn their head to the other side when you approach. Do not worry; these parakeets will also get tame. They simply need a little bit longer to adjust to their new surroundings. **My tip:** Tempt these birds with some foxtail millet. Place half a piece of spray millet at a distance of about 2 inches (5 cm) from the parakeet, so that the bird can see it clearly. You will also need to remain close by, since the purpose of this exercise is for the bird to connect to the surroundings as well as to you in a positive manner.

What You Should Initially Avoid

▶ Excessive and hectic activities around the cage, door slamming, and other loud noises.

▶ Sudden movements, loud talking, screaming, and arguing.

▶ Very bright light, especially in the evening.

- ▶ Direct view of the television, and high volume when it is turned on. Gunshots in cowboy and detective movies are especially frightening for the birds.
- ▶ Do not appear in front of the birds with a changed appearance, such as an unfamiliar head covering.
- ▶ Never point directly at the parakeets with a finger extended. They will fly away in a panic. We do not know why, but possibly they see it as the beak of a bird of prey.
- ▶ Under no circumstances should you grab a parakeet by hand from above. This simulates the attack of a bird of prey, and the parakeet will become scared to death.
- ▶ Cleaning the cage during the first week should be avoided. Excessive handling inside the cage frightens the birds.
- ▶ Complete silence will frighten the birds just as much as screaming noises.

The ABC for an Effortless Adjustment

The involvement of science in the exploration of animals' personalities is relatively young. The results of studies in behavioral biology and neurobiology have forced humans to see animals in a new and different light. This may well be late, but not too late for the well-being of animals. Nearly every animal

TIP

Taking care of the birds during the first few days

To supply the birds with fresh food you need to reach into the cage. Do this in a quiet fashion without hectic movements, even when the birds are frightened and flee from your hand. When that happens, leave the birds alone for a while so that they can settle down again.

Every parakeet has its own personality. Take particular **character differences** into account. Frightened birds require a lot of understanding.

has a personality. How strongly an animal develops its personality varies from one species to the next and is dependent on the complexity of the brain (see page 97). Every one of my parakeets was and is different: Some birds are extremely adventurous and cannot be frightened off by anything. Einstein, a green male parakeet would get great pleasure from scaring my female German Shepherd dog, by landing on her head. The scared dog would take off with flying colors. Psychologically, the bird was far superior to the dog—a small bird, but with a smart head. My other parakeets were much shyer and more restrained. Einstein got his name because of his intelligence and his rapid learning speed. All my birds have a name, and there is a personal story attached to every one of them. Parakeets are personalities with their own character and specific requirements. The most important rule in the human-animal

The plumage colors of parakeets resemble a magnificent color palette.

▼

relationship is to respect the animals' individual traits and characteristics. It facilitates the adjustment and strengthens trust. That also applies to parakeets although they are flock birds. It is hard to believe that a flock consists of so many different personalities. On that point, parakeets are very similar to us. Good bird keepers respect the individuality as well as the inclination toward sociability of their feathered friends.

A "two-edged sword": At this point, I would like to give you a piece of advice, although, to be quite honest, I am not comfortable with it. When you notice that a young parakeet has apparently not yet found a partner for life in a "flock," say, at a breeder's place, a pet shop, or in an animal shelter, then take only one bird for starters. At first sight, this may seem cruel toward the little bird, but in the future, it may benefit from it, because it will be able to fly more and will be quicker to catch. It is also easier to tame a single parakeet. The reason for that is anything but appropriate animal husbandry: As a flock bird, an individual bird always looks for company, but since there are no other parakeets around, it selects—out of necessity—the human as its partner. The younger the bird is, the easier it is for him to accept you. Once that parakeet is tame, you should immediately purchase a second bird. Usually the second bird is faster to tame because it will learn from the first one that you can be trusted.

Taming Parakeets

For parakeets to become hand tamed you have to—once again—show considerable understanding and sensitivity. It is important that you avoid quick, hectic movements and always approach the birds head-on. That is the same way the birds look at you and it allows them to easily recognize you. Commonly occurring events are less likely to frighten the birds. The ice is broken when you succeed in making the birds curious about closer. If the bird remains on its perch, which is usually the case, bring your face to eye level with your bird, and talk and whistle softly. Your behavior will make the bird curious. Under the best of circumstances, the bird will "slide" on its perch closer to you, in order to "investigate" you.

DID YOU KNOW THAT . . .

. . . not every parakeet is a gifted "talker"?

The inclination and talent for "talking" in parakeets is rather variably developed. In general, males—rather than females—are distinctly better at mimicking. A reason for that may be the battle for the favor of a female, because males must imitate the song of their chosen female. The male doing it best is the winner and can then start a family with that female.

you. They must approach you freely and without duress. That is the basic principle of establishing familiarity and applies to all animals, whether it is a lion, a tiger, or a parakeet.

First Step: Creating Curiosity

How can one attract the curiosity of a parakeet? When the bird sits quiet and relaxed on its perch, cautiously approach the closed cage. Avoid any and all loud noises. If the bird moves away from you, remain motionless and whistle softly. After a little while, move

Second Step: Enticing and Tempting

Open the cage door with one hand, holding a piece of spray millet in the other hand. Now the parakeet is alert and watches your movements closely, especially looking at the millet. While doing that, do not forget to talk to the bird and occasionally whistle softly. The bird's attention is focused on the hand holding the millet. The bird feels secure, but is not courageous enough to dare the first steps through the open cage door and toward you. That will take a while!

Third Step: Taking a Critical Step to Overcome a Critical Phase

Wait until the parakeet hops onto the millet. During this critical phase, avoid any disturbing sounds. Withdraw your hand very cautiously—millimeter by millimeter—out of the cage door and in the direction of your body. The parakeet is not supposed to register this movement. Remain a few minutes in this position, and make sure that the bird feeds undisturbed. After a brief trip out of the cage, return your hand cautiously back into the cage. I have had the experience that four to five repetitions of this exercise are sufficient to assure the parakeet that there are no dangers whatsoever outside the cage.

Fourth Step: Journey of Discovery

From the perspective of the parakeet, you are now a sort of good-luck charm. So far, the bird has had only good experiences with you, and so it links you with a positive impression. That is the very basis for the bird to establish trust toward you. Take the parakeet out of the cage again (as described in Step 3). After a little while, the bird will investigate your hands and arms. With your arm extended slightly, the bird will walk toward your shoulder and start nibbling on your hair. All of these little parrots like to do that. Stop at that stage. Do not destroy all the work done by shaking the birds off your arm simply because you do not like that feeling.

MY PET

"Daredevil" or "chicken-hearted"?

During the first few hours the bird is with you, you can already determine the personality. Different types of behavior reveal courage or shyness in the new surroundings, especially when other parakeets are already present.

Start of the test:

Does the parakeet shy away from anything new, for instance, when you attach a bell inside the cage? Does the bird react with screeching when another parakeet approaches? In that case, he has a fearful nature. However, if he is interested in the other parakeets in the cage and walks toward them, he is one of the courageous ones. If the parakeet reacts to your open, quietly extended hand by cautiously touching it with his beak, you have a little "daredevil."

My test results:

These two have a trusting relationship. The bird clearly enjoys being carried around on her hand.

That will destroy the delicate bonds of trust already established.

Fifth Step: The Ice Has Been Totally Broken

Now the trust in you has been significantly fortified, and there is enough courage to explore the environment outside the cage. To make the stimulus even greater, entice your parakeets with objects to nibble on. Newspapers or old calendars and twigs are preferred objects. Try to gently stroke your bird's chest. If he pulls back, try your luck again later.

Most parakeets enjoy this type of establishing contact. Now you experience a very different side of your bird. The shy parakeet has turned into a little explorer who can occasionally be a bit cheeky. Some of my parakeets enjoy immensely chewing on my writing pens when I am inside the aviary recording their behavior.

Note: I cannot emphasize enough how important free flying is for parakeets that do not live in a large aviary (see page 46). However, many bird keepers fear that their birds will not return voluntarily to their cage when they do not feel like it. The answer is simple: Do not offer any food to the birds (or do it at specific locations only outside the cage). Then the birds will readily return to the cage. On the other hand, wild chases will immediately destroy any established trust.

Questions on Maintenance and Settling In

? **Can parakeets be kept together with other animals?** Parakeets are defenseless animals. Their behavior reflects their helplessness: As soon as a particular situation gets too difficult or becomes too confusing, they flee instantly. Parakeets are afraid of dogs and cats. With a lot of patience and understanding, parakeets can be conditioned to a well-trained dog, but close friendships are rare. I must warn you against unsupervised encounters with cats, ferrets, and rats: Birds are included in the innate prey spectrum of these animals, and their hunting instincts cannot really be suppressed in the long term. Moreover, who knows what a parakeet feels when it encounters such potential enemies? It cannot be excluded from possibility that the mere presence of enemies like that creates so much stress for the bird that it will eventually become physically ill, as has been observed in many other animal species. The reason for that is a sudden, dramatic increase in the stress hormone cortisol (hydrocortisone). On the other hand, parakeets are generally ambivalent toward hamsters, mice, and dwarf rabbits. However, for hygienic and medical reasons, I would not keep these animals together with parakeets in the same cage. Other larger birds, especially hookbills like conures, Amazona and the like, are also dangerous if they have access to tiny parakeets.

? **My daughter is seven years old and insists on getting a parakeet. At what age can children accept the responsibility for a parakeet?** I would still wait a year or so, even though this may be hard to convey to a child. Explain to your daughter how sensitive such a small bird is and how much its well-being depends on conscientious care. Cage cleaning, regular food and water, dialogue, and general attention are usually too much for small children. Sometimes they just want to play and do thousands of other things. However, of course there are also exceptions among children. Sometimes they know exactly what their heart desires. Animals are at the focal point of their lives. Is your child one of them? If so, do not hesitate to buy a bird.

? **Three weeks ago, I purchased a second young male for my three-year-old male parakeet. Unfortunately, they do not get along very well. The older one pecks at the younger one. What shall I do?** In your case, patience is required. It is very likely that the two fighting birds will resolve the issues among themselves. Parakeets are flock birds, but in a flock, there is no hierarchy, as there is among chickens and other animals. That facilitates peaceful

coexistence. Presumably, your older bird reacts aggressively toward the younger one because after three years of solitude he no longer remembers the precise rules of life in a flock, and the new bird is a stranger to him. After an extended period of adjustment, the older bird will discover that life as a duo is more interesting. Do not take these arguments too seriously; we too argue among ourselves and children are similarly not squeamish either in their arguments.

? **My parakeet does not want to leave his cage although the cage door is open all day long. Should I take him out of his cage with my hand?** Reaching for a parakeet by hand is actually a "deadly sin." This should really be done only for specific husbandry reasons or in case of disease or illness. When you use your hand, the little parrot feels

like he is in the claws of a bird of prey. He will be afraid of you for a long time. It is better to place a climbing tree directly in front of the cage door, so that the bird can simply hop across. As a particular stimulus, attach a piece of foxtail millet within easy reach on the tree. However, even more important is a bird partner. Parakeets like to explore the world together.

? **I have four parakeets. Three of them behave quite normally, but one is different. The bird lets its head hang down when it is sleeping. Is that normal?** Parakeets are individualists and sometimes they have different sleeping positions. Among my parakeets I have observed the head-down position repeatedly, although the birds were physically and psychologically healthy. I see no reason for concern. Why birds sleep in such an unnatural

position is a mystery to me. I cannot imagine that parakeets in the wild assume such a sleeping position.

? **Early in the morning, my parakeets twitter so loudly that I can no longer sleep. Can I turn off their twittering?** Anybody who keeps parakeets as pets must expect that the birds will twitter loudly. Actually, the happy chirping of birds should put us in a good mood. All birds start their day at first light. Biologically that makes sense: This way they do not lose any time searching for food. Since parakeets in human care do not have to worry about food, you can cover the cage with a cloth or put it in a dark room without feeling guilty about it. I am sure that in time the parakeets will adjust to such a rhythm.

Nutrition

Parakeets that live with us usually have an ample supply
of food. However, it is not only the amount that is important,
but especially the quality and variety.

Correct Nutrition— an Important Subject

The principal component in a healthy parakeet diet is a seed mixture made up of different types of seeds. However, fresh food, such as green feed, fruit, and vegetables must be included if your little parrots are to remain healthy.

The carousel of life revolves around food and sexuality. This applies to nearly all living beings, but especially to parakeets.

Male Parakeets Remain Slim

Why do female parakeets that live under our care have a propensity toward obesity? To answer this question, we have to deal with the biology and the evolution of parakeets. In the course of millions of years, living beings have adapted to the environment, especially to the availability of food. This guarantees that the diversity of creatures can use all available food resources. There are specialists, like the giant panda that feeds exclusively on bamboo, or omnivores, like us and mammals such as pigs, as well as plant feeders (herbivores) like parakeets. Of course, the adaptation takes place at different levels, and one of these is the behavioral level. Back to parakeets now and to the question of why female parakeets are inclined to become obese in captivity. The production and incubation of eggs requires a lot of energy from the female. Her male partner provides a large portion of this energy, i.e., food, to her. He feeds the female in a totally dedicated fashion during the courtship. He continuously flies out looking for food and then carries what he has found back to the female. He virtually stuffs the food down the female's beak. The biological purpose of all this is to prepare the female for the energy consuming production and subsequent laying of eggs. This guarantees that the female gets sufficient food and does not lose any energy from any unnecessary search for food. This interaction works very well in nature; however, with parakeets kept as pets, difficulties can arise.

This is an excellent way for a bird to quench its thirst. However, you should exercise caution with narrow, tall, water-filled containers, where a bird can easily drown if it falls in.

Reduced energy consumption: Only the smallest number of parakeet hens is permitted to breed, so most of them avoid energy-consuming egg production. Yet, parakeet pairs are still forming. The male feeds the female and she accepts the food, just as in nature, but eggs are not laid and progeny are not being reared. In addition to her own search for food, the female receives of domesticated parakeets. The results are surprising: The average energy consumption of one parakeet is nearly 50 times as much as that of a human, when prorated to grams of body mass (humans 175 pounds [80 kg], parakeets 1.75 ounces [50 g]). Obviously, then, males that were feeding their females had an even higher energy consumption. Parakeets are virtual gluttons. On average—depending upon prevailing conditions—they take in .4–.5 ounces (12–14 g) of food. That would mean

juvenile birds already have food preferences?

Just like birds in the wild, our pet birds learn during their youth what plants are edible and which ones are not. Once they are adults, they can rarely ever be persuaded to eat a new type of food. Many bird keepers complain that their parakeets take only a certain type of seed mixture and even refuse high-quality fruit. Therefore, it is important to give young birds a highly variable diet.

additional rations. That is what leads to obesity. Another reason is that the male uses up more energy by flying more to gather food. It would be wrong—although not lethal—to put such a female on a diet. Birds in general have a much higher metabolism than mammals. They require enormous amounts of energy within a short period of time. Therefore, our small parrots are not very likely to starve to death when in our care.

Food requirement: A recent study was conducted to investigate the feeding behavior and daily energy consumption that a man with a weight of 175 pounds (80 kg) would need 44 pounds (20 kg) of food per day. During the summer months, there is a substantial weight gain in parakeets. Why that is so, no one knows yet. Maybe the reason is that the home of parakeets is in the southern half of the Earth. Could it be possible that a different seasonal rhythm has become embedded in their genes? I do not know, but I suspect it is so, because my birds are breeding most successfully in November. However, as I said, those are my experiences, and they may well be a random occurrence.

Your parakeets need a lot of **exercise** so that they do not get too fat. Faily free flight in your home is a must for the little parrots.

Naturally slender: How can female parakeets maintain a slender figure? For parakeets, the slimming cure is called . . . flying (see Parakeets Must Fly, page 46). For your female parakeets to maintain a normally trim figure there is—in addition to ample flying exercise—yet another effective method, suggested by Antoine Schnegg. Permit the female to incubate for a certain length of time and then remove the eggs. Although this may be harsh for the progeny, it is better for the well-being of the hen.

What Do Wild Parakeets Feed On?

Not only is the amount of food decisive for the health of a bird, but so is the variety. The "wild" parrots of Australia show us what a healthy diet for our pets should be. The menu of the ancestors is a guideline to the food plan of today. For details about this, we are indebted to the zoologist Edmund Wyndham, who has studied the natural history of parakeets in their native habitat. Their dietary plan contains the seeds from 21 different plant species—a rather impressive number. The majority of these plants belong to the grasses. To list all of these would be too comprehensive. Instead, I would like to list only the four plants wild parakeets feed on most frequently: *Astrebla lappacea*, *Astrebla pectinata*, *Atriplex angulata*, and *Boerhavia triplex*. The birds feed on those plants that grow after the onset of the rainy season, and they are not very selective. This enables them to survive during the harsh months. When nature provides food in abundance, however, parakeets have certain preferences, as well as individual tastes.

Free-living parakeets can always feed on fresh seeds that contain all essential nutrients. The situation is different with parakeets that are kept as pets. Our birds are armed against deficiency syndromes only when they have been fed a balanced (varied) diet from early in their lives. Parakeets that have been given a monotonous diet are difficult to convert to other food items later on.

Small treats are allowed occasionally.

Seeds as Staple Food

Seeds from different plant species form a significant part of parakeets' diets. **Note:** Manufactured diets are also an important part of nutrition for parakeets. Avian veterinarians routinely recommend that caged birds be offered pellets or extruded foods intended for the species. A balanced diet for parakeets should include a helping of one of these diets along with a serving of seeds, fruits, and vegetables. A diet consisting mainly, or only of, seeds may result in a vitamin A deficiency. Be sure to contact your veterinarian with specific questions regarding your bird's diet.

Healthy mixture: A high-quality seed mixture consists of 30% canary seed, 25% silver millet, 20% Plata and Senegal millet, 15% oat groats and hairy crabgrass, 5% Niger (or Nyjer) seed, and 5% linseed. Often good mixtures also contain Cardinal seeds and Perilla seeds as well as Japanese (Duck) millet. Most of these seeds are available from seed shops, less often from pet shops. A basic parakeet diet can also be purchased premixed. Food manufacturers are producing balanced mixtures according to their own recipes, and they will often supplement that with iodine salts. I have had good experiences with premixed, commercial diets.

Use-by date: Check the use-by date at the time of purchase. The seed plants for use in bird feeds are usually harvested once a year. With appropriate storage, these seeds are capable of germination until the next sowing season. The shelf life is about one year, although the nutrient and vitamin content will gradually diminish.

Storage: Decisive for the nutrient content of seeds is the type of storage used. Seeds should always be stored in dark, well-ventilated rooms. From the time of packing, seeds will get very little air; therefore, make sure that the mixture is not older than four to five months.

Germination test: Take a teaspoon of grains from a package and soak them in a little bit of water. The water should cover all grains to a depth of about $3/4$ inch(2 cm). Wait for 24 hours, and then rinse the seeds in a strainer with lukewarm water and place them in a shallow glass. The bottom of the container should be covered with a damp paper towel. The seeds must not be covered airtight during germination; otherwise, they will quickly be covered by fungi. After 24 hours, they can be fed to the birds as soaked seeds and after 48 hours as germinated seeds. If only a few of the seeds have germinated, they are too old and are no longer suitable as high-quality food. Feed germinated seeds in a special bowl and remove any leftovers after an hour or two.

Amount of seeds: Each day, you should feed two tablespoons of seeds per parakeet. Check whether this quantity is sufficient. A parakeet that is kept correctly will eat only as much as it needs. Under no circumstances should you ration the basic diet to protect the birds against obesity. Watch for empty husks: many a parakeet has starved, although it was sitting in front of a presumed mountain of food. Parakeets feed only on the seed kernel inside the husk. The latter is simply dropped while the kernel is swallowed. To an inexperienced bird keeper, these empty husks can create the impression of a full seed bowl, a tragic assumption that has been fatal for many parakeets.

Healthy Diet—
at a Glance

The mixture. ▶

The quality of the seed mixture is—of course—of principal importance in a healthy parakeet diet. However, green feed, such as dandelions, chickweed, and herbs, are part of a variable diet, along with pellets and extruded foods.

◀ Vegetables and fruit.

These contain important vitamins, oils, and minerals. You need to experiment to see what your parakeets prefer. Offer two to three types of green feed to your birds daily. Fruit and vegetables must be cut into small pieces before feeding.

Treats. ▶

All parakeets love spray millet. I give a small piece every day to my birds, because it is a high-quality food. With sufficient flying exercise, the birds will not put on any extra weight.

Nutritional Building Blocks

The correct composition of the diet is of paramount importance for all living beings including parakeets. To remain healthy, these little parrots require protein, carbohydrates, fats, and minerals.

Parakeets like all animals, require protein, carbohydrates, and fats. These three nutrient substances have different tasks within the body, but one thing is common to all of them: They produce energy. By the way, it is a mistake to believe that vitamins and minerals also provide energy.

Protein Ensures Renewal

Protein provides about half the energy that fat does. Consequently, one could think that an "energy consumer" like the parakeet principally consumes fatty foods. That is only half the truth, because protein also plays a major part in renewal. This can readily be demonstrated by the following example: When you look at yourself in the mirror, and do so again a month later, nearly all skin cells will have been replaced by new ones. Only a few cells have survived and new, permanent cells have developed. Cell death and the birth of new cells is a constant process. Newly developed cells require protein. This is a biological principle that also applies to parakeets.

Insufficient amounts of protein in the diet leads to deficiency syndromes or ultimately to the demise of an organism. Why does the lack of protein have such significant consequences? Very simple: Muscles consist largely of protein. According to studies conducted, the diet of parakeets' should contain about 10% protein, because the feathers, the beak, and the claws consist of virtually pure protein.

During the molt (change of feathers), parakeets require two to three times as much protein. During that period it is advisable to give more canary seeds and oat groats (coarsely ground-up, dehusked cereal grains, mostly oats), because these seeds contain a lot of protein. Here are some details about the protein content in 2.2 pounds (1 kg) of fresh seeds from the following plants: white millet = 4 ounces (115 g), red millet = 4 ounces (115 g), canary seed = 5.4 ounces (156 g), groats = 4.7 ounces (135 g).

Carbohydrates Provide the Fuel

Among the best-known carbohydrates are starch and sugar. These are contained in bread, pasta, and sweets (among many other items).

Carbohydrates are the fuel and energy supplier, respectively, for parakeets. Parakeets can tap these energy sources readily, because plant seeds contain principally starch. With the aid of their beaks, the little parrots peel the

A "bed" inside some cat grass. The parakeet is nibbling on the fresh grass.

seed, swallow the kernel, and drop indigestible husks. A total of 2.2 pounds (1 kg) of fresh seeds from the following seed plants contain starch in these amounts: white millet = 1.4 pounds (712 g), red millet = 1.3 pounds (699 g), canary seed = 1.2 pounds (615 g), groats = 1.4 pounds (707 g). Consequently, our parakeets never suffer from carbohydrate deficiency.

Fat — Sheer Energy

Butter, margarine, and oils are nearly pure fats. The tasks of fats in animal bodies are diverse. Among other things, they provide energy and the transportation means for some vitamins. For instance, vitamin A dissolves in fat. The respective amounts required by animals varies from one species to the next. Polar bears and seals require a lot of fat, but parakeets on the other hand, need more carbohydrates. The amount of fat in white millet, for instance, is 1.2 ounces (35 g), in red millet it is 1.3 ounces (38 g), in canary seed it is 2 ounces (56 g), and in groats it is 2.3 ounces (66 g). **Note:** One gram of fat provides twice the amount of calories of carbohydrates and protein. Female parakeets have a tendency toward obesity, so they should get foods that are low in fat. For instance, I rarely give my parakeets sunflower seeds, because they contain too much fat. Other fatty treats should also be fed only sparingly.

Minerals Ensure Well-being

Many people are uncertain about what exactly minerals are. Moreover, incorrect information is disseminated frequently. Minerals are the salts (e.g., cooking salt, often iodized, and limestone) of various metals. The body takes up these salts; however, most pure metals are very toxic, even in small amounts.

I have recently encountered the consequences of an incorrect definition of minerals myself. The camels in an animal enclosure suffered from copper deficiency, according to the diagnosis of the treating veterinarian. The reaction of the animal keepers was swift. They offered copper rods for the camels to lick. That was highly inappropriate, because pure copper is very toxic. Fortunately, the camels rejected the "offer." All living beings require minerals, which have diverse tasks to fulfill. Without minerals, metabolism does not function properly. What is important, however, is a balance—not too much or too little.

DIET PLAN FOR YOUR PARAKEETS

GIVE YOUR BIRDS DAILY . . .

Fresh seeds:	two teaspoons per parakeet. Make sure this amount is sufficient if your birds get a lot of exercise.
Fresh water:	must always be available in sufficient quantity
Green feed (seasonal):	e.g., dandelions, chickweed, shepherd's purse, plantain, ryegrass, and herbs such as parsley, basil, or cress
Branches with budding leaves:	e.g., willow, birch, poplar, linden (basswood), conifers
Vegetables, according to season:	broccoli, cauliflower, carrots, cucumbers, kohlrabi, spinach, zucchini, lettuce, endive lettuce
Fruit, according to season:	apples, pears, apricots, bananas, grapefruit, grapes, oranges
Spray millet:	a small piece

Note: Treats should be given only once a week. Make sure the treats contain as little sugar and honey as possible.

Parakeets have a high metabolic rate. They must **never go hungry.** It is better to avoid fatty treats and provide more free-flying opportunities.

It has been estimated that parakeets require somewhere between .6 and 1 percent of the daily food rations in calcium salts. Parakeets cannot really cover their mineral requirement through the intake of seeds. Therefore, it is important to provide cuttlebones and other mineral supplements. Minerals must always be freely available to the birds.

Note: It has been a mystery for a long time why wild macaws (the large relatives of parakeets) in Peru were regularly seen along rocky cliffs, feeding on soil. Now we know that it is their way of covering their mineral requirement, and at the same time neutralizing and detoxifying their excessively acidic stomach contents. I offer my parakeets dandelion, shepherd's purse, and other plants, including roots. My birds like to pick through the soil, curiously investigating every bit of it.

Vitamins Are Essential for the Metabolism

Vitamins are substances that cannot be produced by the body. Humans and animals need to take in small amounts with their food. Vitamins, or at least their active ingredients, are produced by plants. Without vitamins, essential metabolic processes of the body are interrupted. Vitamin deficiency leads to diseases. How many vitamins a parakeet needs depends on the individual and on its physical performance and physiological requirements, such as the molt, growth, and reproduction. The small amounts of vitamins involved can be illustrated based on vitamin A. According to scientific studies, a parakeet requires only 1/12000th g daily. Therefore, it is very important to give precisely the required amount when administering vitamin drops. Also very important is the storage of vitamins, which are very sensitive to environmental conditions. Vitamins are destroyed by heat, oxygen, UV light, or through the influence of acids. Since plant seeds contain vitamins only in very small amounts—or none at all—you must also give green feed to your birds. Green plants and carrots contain the essential vitamins. The most thoroughly investigated vitamins for birds are vitamin A, vitamin B complex, vitamin D, and vitamin E. There are other vitamins, but to mention all of them here would go beyond the scope of this book. Here, in an abridged form, are the roles of each vitamin mentioned above, so that you are aware how important these are for your birds.

▸ **Vitamin A:** facilitates growth and enhances the immune system. It dissolves only in fat, and thus cannot be administered in water.

▸ **Vitamin B complex:** a group of vitamins that assist in the metabolism of various substances in the body. For instance, without their aid, food substances cannot be metabolized. Vitamin B_1 plays a role in nerve cell function. A deficiency of it leads to paralysis in the legs and claws, and the parakeets can no longer firmly grasp perches. Sadly, that marks the onset of a frightening disease picture.

▶ **Vitamin D:** important for bone structure. A deficiency leads to rachitis, a disease whereby the bones are not sufficiently hardened. Vitamin D is formed by sunlight. Therefore, the parakeets should have access to a sunny location. However, windows filter out a lot of the healthy rays, so supplemental lighting should be provided and can be purchased in many pet stores and home improvement centers. Look for those labeled "full spectrum" lights.

▶ **Vitamin E:** important for fertility and for protein—carbohydrate and fat metabolism. Birds require more vitamin E than mammals.

Note: Deficiency syndromes are extremely rare when you feed your birds appropriately. During spring and summer, vitamins are in abundance in young plants and cereal grains. Therefore, I do not give vitamin supplements during the summer. However, in the winter, when there is less sun, I supplement green feed with a multivitamin preparation available from pet shops.

Green Feed Is Part of the Diet Plan

Your parakeets require green feed on a regular basis. This type of food contains essential oils, vitamins, and minerals. However, the green feed available is not always the same nutritionally. Especially young plants have a higher nutrient and vitamin content. Therefore, it is always advisable to include fresh, young plants in the diet.

I have outlined the diet plan for my small birds' flock below. Of course, many other combinations are possible. For instance, there is a new food plant available (in pet shops and other places), that is very popular with parakeets. It is available under the name Golliwoog or Creeping Inch plant (*Callisia repens*) (see photograph, page 36). Depending on the season, I feed the following green and plant food mixture.

Wild plants: chickweed, plantain, dandelion, shepherd's purse, sorrel, watercress, oat weed, common meadow grass, and perennial ryegrass

Lettuce: Head lettuce, endive lettuce, and romain lettuce

Vegetables and herbs: basil, parsley, spinach, fennel, sweet balm, cucumber, broccoli, pumpkin, capsicum (paprika), celery, kohlrabi, tomatoes, and carrots

◀ *Fresh branches with leaves and/or leaf buds not only are eaten eagerly, but also provide hours of activity.*

Fruit: apple, pineapple, pear, apricot, grapes, raspberries, and kiwifruit
Caution: Plants used as parakeet food must not be collected along roads. Exhaust fumes have contaminated these plants. Avoid areas where herbicides and pesticides have been used. Also, be careful not to feed your parakeet the following unhealthy and/or toxic foods: avocado (toxic!), raw potatoes, lemon, rhubarb, plum, and cabbage.

Dinner Is Served

How do you feed parakeets? That is certainly a strange question: Most parakeets get their food in a bowl (for hygienic reasons). However, if one were to ask the birds, they would rather prefer their food being offered the way their wild relatives find it. Feeding is a social act for parakeets. As soon as one of them starts to feed, all the other ones will follow. That is exactly the way it happens in my aviary.
Seeds: I scatter the seeds along the bottom so that the small parrots have to look for their food and then pick it up. There is also a full seed bowl in the aviary. When given a choice, the flock will walk along the ground, picking up the seeds as they move along. The seed bowl is used only to "top off" if the birds are still hungry. Of course, you cannot scatter seeds along the floor in your house, but what you can do is offer the seeds in two or three shallow bowls scattered around the room. That may not be quite the same as the joint feeding of the entire flock, but it does promote the birds' curiosity. Just to clarify, the seed bowls are intended only as extra rations. They are no substitute for the full seed bowl in the cage.

CHECKLIST

Feeding Rules

To keep your parakeets healthy, it is essential that you comply with the following rules:

- ○ Store dry food (seeds) in a dark and well-ventilated place.

- ○ Check the use-by date of commercially packed foods.

- ○ Remove empty seed husks from the seed bowl by blowing across the seed dish.

- ○ Rinse green feed, fruit, and vegetables several times with lukewarm water before use.

- ○ Do not feed wilted or partially decayed green feed to your birds. Spoiled food can cause intestinal problems and diarrhea.

- ○ Do not offer a frozen or very cold food to your birds.

- ○ Cut fruit and vegetables, so that the birds find it easier to select smaller parts, and remove all leftover food in the evening, or within 2 hours if the room is warm, to avoid spoilage.

- ○ Fresh drinking water must always be available.

- ○ Fatty treats should not be given more than once a week.

- ○ Spicy foods from your dining table are NOT parakeet food.

MY PET

Food preferences of your parakeet

Parakeets are no culinary experts, but they can still develop preferences. Distribute small bowls with fruit, lettuce, and vegetables throughout the room.

The test starts:

Send your candidate out in search of his favorite food. Hide the little bowls so that they cannot be seen at first glance. Now observe several times in a row which bowl the bird approaches first during three or four attempts. If he flies to the same bowl the first two times, it could be a coincidence, because he has to learn first where his favorite food is.

My test results:

Fruit and vegetables: Distribute fruit and vegetables in small slices so the birds find it easier to pick out suitable pieces.

Green feed: You should offer fresh leaves, either in a food bowl or in small bunches that are tied to the sides of the cage. This way, the birds have to "work" for their food, which then also provides some exercise.

Nibbling Food

Natural branches are essential for parakeets. The birds love to gnaw on them, and they provide valuable minerals and vitamins. Parakeets prefer branches from willow, linden (basswood), poplar, birch, ash, conifer, and hazelnut trees.

Chewing on branches can also stop the beak from becoming excessively long, which spares the birds a trip to the veterinarian, but it won't necessarily stop the beak from becoming overgrown.

Something Tasty for In-between

For most parakeets, spray millet is a real hit. The usual recommendation is to feed spray millet only sparingly, because this type of seed is rather fatty. Yet, this millet is highly nutritious, and it can also be used to nurse weak and sick birds back to health. Therefore, I suggest that birds be given a small piece of spray millet every day. If your parakeets get sufficient exercise, this will not affect their weight. My 28 birds get six to eight spikes of spray millet every day. Occasionally, you can also treat your birds—in good conscience—with a nibbling stick of kiwi and other fruit and seeds. Nevertheless, keep in mind that such treats are indeed caloric heavyweights and must be given only very sparingly.

The Right Drink

Make sure your parakeets get fresh drinking water daily. Their water requirement is dependent upon temperature, humidity, and food. Some types of food contain more water and others less. Under scientifically standardized conditions, a parakeet requires 3 to 5 ml water per day in conjunction with a normal diet. That looks like very little; however, when one considers that its circulatory system contains only 6 ml of blood, it is not that little. A human being with 5 to 6 quarts (5–6 l) of blood usually does not take in more than 3 quarts (3 l) of water a day.

Toxic and Dangerous

The tamer a parakeet is, the cheekier the bird gets. Parakeets will nibble with great enthusiasm on plants, pencils, and ballpoint pens, and will not even stop in front of small batteries. Therefore, you will need to remove all harmful and toxic objects from the parakeet room (see Checklist, page 37). Whether a particular indoor plant is toxic for parakeets is not always known. When in doubt . . . remove the plant. The following plants are detrimental to the health of parakeets: avocado, Aaron, Christ's thorn, Christmas rose, Dieffenbachia, ivy, yew tree, foxglove, laburnum, fool's parsley, hyacinth, petty spurge, lobelia, laurel, mistletoe, lilies of the valley, narcissus, oleander, primrose, larkspur, sun spurge, thorn apple, belladonna, poinsettia.

Similarly, plants with spines and thorns (e.g., cacti and holly) should be inaccessible to parakeets. The birds could sustain serious injuries when they come into contact with these plants.

A special fresh-food plate for parakeets. This is the life!

Well Cared-for and Perfectly Happy

A clean home and proper care are the be-all and end-all for the health of your parakeets. If, in spite of that, one of your birds should get sick, do not hesitate to take him to a veterinarian immediately.

Cleanliness Is the First Commandment

Incorrect husbandry (care) and dirty cages or aviaries cause most diseases. Therefore, you must clean the cage and aviary at regular intervals. Your parakeets will show their appreciation by remaining healthy.

Hygiene is of paramount importance in nature. Only very rarely do we find areas in the wild that are soiled by fecal matter and similar dirt, because it is broken down and recycled. Cleaning armies in the form of microorganisms are constantly on the move. Hygiene is a matter of survival and guarantees the continued existence of an animal species. However, when the balance of microorganisms is disturbed, the number of disease-causing organisms increases, endangering the animals. Anyone who accepts nature as a teacher will quickly understand why cages and aviaries must be cleaned regularly.

Preening—An Important Matter

Extensive care of the plumage is an innate behavior that takes up a lot of time every day. When you watch your parakeets, you will notice that in the course of the day, they spend several hours preening. Of course, this does not occur continuously; however, nearly every activity the birds engage in, whether feeding, sleeping, or involvement with a partner, is always concluded with a few minutes of preening.

The reason for this is a matter of survival: Flying becomes difficult with soiled feathers that stick together. With a flying speed of about 28 mph (42 km/h), parakeets use up the smallest amount of oxygen, and with that there is minimum energy consumption. However, the latter is possible only when the plumage is in top shape, i.e., perfectly clean. Moreover, a properly cared-for plumage also protects against cold and wetness.

The beak of a parakeet serves as its multipurpose cleaning device, with which the bird keeps every single feather of its attractive plumage in top

The beak and tongue are the two most important "tools" for preening plumage.

2 Danger of injury. Blood vessels that extend into the claw can be damaged when the claws are trimmed. It is best if the veterinarian shows you first how it is done.

1 Trimming the claws. This is always an unpleasant procedure for the birds. Being picked up by a human hand always creates a lot of fear.

3 Bathing. A bath among wet lettuce leaves is not a bad idea. Occasionally, you should give your birds that opportunity.

condition. The bird meticulously smooths its feathers and removes every dirt particle, as well as dust. With acrobatic agility, the bird turns and twists to reach the long tail and wing feathers and then slide them through its beak. Even the naked feet and toes are nibbled on to remove skin scales and dirt. Only the head and neck region are worked over using the toes. Similarly, scratching is part of the body care. It can be considered as a sort of "precleaning" that supplements preening the plumage with the beak. However, with this the parakeet demonstrates a special characteristic, as was observed by the American biologist Barbara Brockway. The bird uses the longest toe and claw to scratch its head, but, for lateral body parts and the cloaca, the bird uses the joint between the metatarsus (midfoot)

and toe. This is a very clever arrangement, because it protects the bird against injury in the cloacal region.

Caring for Your Birds

When looking after parakeets you barely ever have to handle them physically. However, you need to monitor them daily. This is the only way you will be able to detect disease symptoms early.

Claws: Check the length of the claws regularly. Excessively long claws can be dangerous for the bird. They may become entangled in cloth, wire mesh, or narrow cracks. Ask your veterinarian to show you how to trim the claws. If you decide to trim the claws yourself, take the bird into one hand as shown in the photograph above. Hold the individual toes against a bright light. The blood vessels inside the horny part of the toe are then clearly visible. Cut the horny section of the claw (just below the blood vessels) from above, obliquely downward (see Tip, below). Natural perches are usually abrasive enough to keep the claws short.

Beak: The birds' beaks serve as knife, fork, and spoon. In fact, they also use it as a "third foot" while climbing. The point of the beak sometimes chips off in thin layers, which is not unusual. It is a normal process of gradual beak renewal. However, it does become problematic when the beak has grown too long. Especially in males, the upper beak sometimes grows excessively fast. There may be diverse reasons for this and sometimes there may even be serious disease involved (see page 87). Whatever the cause, the beak will need to be trimmed. Beaks that are too long are a severe problem for the birds, and I advise you to have a veterinarian attend to this.

Note: Often the reason for excessive growth of the beak is a lack of sufficient gnawing material, meaning the birds are then unable to grind their beaks. Therefore you need to provide branches and twigs for your parakeets to gnaw on (see page 78). Concrete perches are also helpful in keeping toenails and beaks in good shape.

Cage Maintenance

Daily: Seed bowls must be washed out daily with hot water and subsequently dried. Make sure there are no old leftover seeds rotting in the cage. These are ideal breeding grounds for fungi, bacteria, and unicellular organisms.

Weekly: Once a week the cage needs to be cleaned thoroughly. Remove perches and toys from the cage; everything must be washed and scrubbed under hot (!) water. Do not use cleaning agents! Remove the dried-on fecal material to avoid the transmission of bacteria and viruses. Remove all the old bird substrate and replace it completely with a fresh cage liner.

Monthly: Once a month the entire cage, including the bottom tray, is rinsed off with hot water and thoroughly dried.

Note: Do not forget to clean the other places that are popular with your parakeets, such as the bird tree or the various favorite landing spots throughout the room.

Cleaning the Aviary

How often you clean your aviary, depends, of course, on its size and the number of birds that are being kept in it. The following care plan has proven

TIP

Injury while trimming the claws

When the claws of your birds have become too long, you should have a veterinarian show you how to trim them. However, if—in spite of all precautions—a blood vessel in the claw has been damaged and a drop of blood emerges, it should be stopped with styptic powder. But, you should ask a veterinarian how to properly stop the bleeding; there are several packaged products that can help and are intended for use with birds.

Saying Good-bye

My eight-year-old son loves our two parakeets, Nicki and Pia, very much. Unfortunately, both of them are already 10 years old and with that, they are well into their senior age. What is the best way to console our son when the birds die?

It always hurts when a beloved person or a beloved animal that has lived for many years in the family dies. Parakeets as pets can live 10 to 15 years. When your two birds have been happy and healthy for 10 years, one can assume that they have had a happy life with you. That is a good starting position to prepare your son gently for the death of his beloved birds. The death of a living being is part of life and an inescapable fact. However, it gives some consolation if one knows that a life—in this case that of your parakeets—was fulfilled and a good one.

Allow mourning

Most likely, your two parakeets are not going to die at the same time, but one first and then the other. Let your son mourn for his dead parakeet. It is not a good idea to return immediately to daily events or to go out on the same day to buy a "replacement bird." The parakeet that is left behind will also mourn for his partner. Maybe you can get him a new partner in the days to come—ideally, you should make that two young birds, so that you don't once again have a single bird remaining when the other parakeet dies.

Bury the bird

For most people it is consoling when they can visit the gravesite of a beloved person or an animal. Therefore, you and your son should bury the parakeet. A parakeet can be buried in your garden or yard. If you do not own a garden or yard, you can have the bird buried in a pet cemetery or cremated at an animal crematorium. Such a farewell ritual is incredibly important for children, because this way they can better handle such a sad event. Afterward, they can visit the little gravesite frequently, and maintain and decorate it with flowers, so that they can still show their dedication to their dead feathered friend.

to be effective for my aviary, which holds 28 parakeets.

Note: While most parakeet owners do not keep their birds in an aviary, the following information is helpful to people who keep a large number of parakeets.

Daily: Rinse out seed bowls daily or at least several times week with hot water, and dry thoroughly. Within the aviary, select sites for seed and water bowls that are protected against bird droppings. After all, a parakeet drops a fecal ball every 15 to 25 minutes. Fecal material in water or food is a dangerous infection source for diseases. Remove all fresh-food leftovers.

Weekly: Remove fecal material from the bird sand. **My tip:** Buy a large strainer for that job and sift all soiled sand. The fecal balls will be caught in the strainer and the sand will fall on through. This is the best way to clean the sand. You will need to use a brush to remove fecal matter from perches and other items in the aviary.

Monthly: Once a month there will have to be a major cleanup in the aviary. The bird sand needs to be replaced completely. Old branches and twigs are removed and replaced by new ones. The fixed perches are cleaned off with a wire brush and hot water.

The Molt

Many bird keepers become frightened when their birds suddenly lose their feathers. There is no reason to get upset. In fact, it is a natural process whereby old feathers are being replaced by new ones. This change of feathers is referred to as the molt. The molt is not a disease. However, during this phase the parakeets are susceptible to diseases. In any case, the parakeets should be particularly protected against temperature changes, drafts, and stress during the molt.

Unlike birds in the wild, the molt of pet parakeets is not tied to a particular season. Indeed, a change of plumage can

Body care as a twosome. This is a lot more fun than doing it alone. ▶

occur several times a year, and yet healthy parakeets do not have any problems with that. They only preen themselves more frequently. You can give them some help by using commercial products specially designed as "molt aids" (calcium- and phosphate-enriched products), commonly available from pet shops. You should closely monitor the condition of the plumage. It becomes particularly attractive and shiny when the parakeets are given ample opportunity to spread their wings and fluff up when it is raining. The rain will penetrate all the way to the skin and so wash away tiny dust particles.

Exposure to a rain shower is for birds very similar to a daily shower for us. When the first raindrops fall, my parakeet flock will leave the dry area of the aviary and clearly enjoy the natural rain shower—every bird to its own taste, some more and others less. Afterward, the plumage is intensively preened. Give your indoor birds a similar pleasure during the warmer season of the year. Simply place the cage with the birds (but without food) outside for at least 15 minutes when there is gentle rain falling. Do not worry; your birds will not catch a cold when they are subsequently placed in a draft-free room. Be cautious to the danger of other animals who could attack your parakeet, debris, or other things like animal or wild bird feces entering the cage.

MY PET

Is your parakeet maintaining its weight?

A parakeet's weight is an indicator of its health. If the parakeet is not visibly overweight and "maintains its figure," this is a good sign. However, if the bird loses several grams within a relatively short period, you should monitor it closely.

The test starts:

Weigh your parakeet on a kitchen scale. That is easier than you think. Place a little seed dish with some foxtail millet on the scale. Weigh the bowl, including content, and record the weight. Have the bird sitting on your hand and carefully take your bird to the scale. When the parakeet is hungry, it will not hesitate to hop onto the scale. Then you record the weight. If it remains more or less the same, everything is okay.

My test results:

Common Diseases

Parakeets are quiet patients and a disease is not easily noticed in them. Therefore, it is important that you check your birds closely every day. If you notice a problem, only immediate treatment will save the life of these little parrots, in most instances.

Parakeets, just like their wild cousins in Australia, are rather robust birds, but they can also get sick. Therefore, it is important to check the birds closely every day and contact your veterinarian immediately at the first sign of a disease.

"Difficult" Patients

For a veterinarian, parakeets are difficult patients. The reason is that the birds are very small and have an enormously high metabolic rate. A few numbers can underline that point: The heart weighs about .58 g (the human heart is about 11 ounces/300 g). The parakeet heart, little more than half a gram heavy, beats an incredible 300 to 500 times a minute (see page 12). The blood volume varies from 4 to 6 ml. If blood is taken from such a tiny animal, every single drop counts. That is very difficult work for a veterinarian. It is not surprising, then, that some of them may think too much is expected of them. To look after the health of your bird, search for a veterinarian or avian veterinarian who has experience with parakeets. Do not waste time, because the life of such a small bird can easily be threatened.

How to Recognize Disease Symptoms

It is not easy to recognize whether a parakeet is ill. With that in mind, here are a few external changes that may suggest an illness:

▸ Is the bird sleepy, less active, and tending to withdraw?
▸ Has its feeding behavior changed? Does the bird drink more water than before? Is the feces more watery and has it changed color?
▸ Does the parakeet defecate less than before?
▸ Does the bird sit in the corner of the cage with the plumage fluffed up?
▸ Does it have a runny nose? Are its eyes swollen?
▸ Is the bird regurgitating mucus from its crop?
▸ Is its plumage dull and matted?

First Steps When an Illness Is Suspected

Remove the sick parakeet from all the other birds in the cage or aviary. Place it in a separate cage so that it can neither hear nor see the other birds. That will protect the sick bird against stress and the other birds from also becoming infected. The temporary separation of the bird partner must be accepted.

Moreover, the sick bird is usually so weak that other birds around it would only be a disturbing factor.

Monitor how much the sick bird is eating (if it is eating at all) and drinking and whether it has diarrhea. Heat lamps—as a first aid measure—have accomplished wonders with some of my parakeets. Suitable infrared lamps (200 watt) are available from pet or electrical goods shops. Place such a lamp approximately 20 inches (50 cm) from the cage. The lamp should shine on only half the cage, so that the parakeet can choose which temperature is acceptable.

The Trip to the Veterinarian

Transport your birds in an "infirmary cage." Avoid stress, such as noise and hectic activities. Remove seed and drink containers. Wrap a blanket around the cage.

Note: Do not clean the cage, so that the veterinarian can take fecal samples, if need be.

Skin and Feather Diseases

These types of diseases can have many different causes. Frequently, parasites have attacked the skin directly. These are known as ectoparasites (external parasites). However, metabolic disorders of internal organs or parasites that live inside an animal (endoparasites) can also be the cause of skin diseases. Ectoparasitic attacks are often caused by husbandry and nutritional mistakes. The most common ectoparasites are mites, animal lice (*Mallophaga*), and fungi.

Mites

Mites can be dangerous for parakeets. These parasites belong to the group of spiderlike animals (*Arthropoda*), and feed on skin particles and lymphatic fluid.

Burrowing mite (*Sarcoptes*): This parasite burrows strainerlike passages into the skin and into the beak of parakeets. The bird's body reacts to such invasions with a horny growth. This type of mite infestation is referred to as parakeet mange, also called scaly face and leg mite. Skin mites (*Cnemidocoptes*) can be living inside the body of a bird since its nestling time. However, only after the body has become weakened by stress will they start to damage the bird. Once parakeet mange breaks out on one bird, you should immediately contact your veterinarian. The affected part(s) must be treated for several days with a special solution from the veterinarian. This treatment closes up the burrowing and feeding passages of the burrowing mite so that the parasite dies. Because mange occurs only in weakened birds, the parakeets' general condition must always be closely monitored, and the birds should be provided with vitamin preparations administered through the drinking water. If the parakeets' feet are affected by mange, and if the parakeets' leg is banded, the ring must be removed. Any swelling could lead to blood vessel blockages and the subsequent die-off of the banded leg.

Red Bird Mite: This mite attacks birds only at night and sucks out their blood. When this happens, the bird becomes rather unsettled. Brooding females and chicks are constantly under threat from the Red Bird Mite (*Dermanyssus gallinae*), because it is always dark inside the nest box. In adult birds, such constant blood drainage can lead to anemia. Chicks can be weakened to such a

2 **Cotton swabs** are very useful, for instance for applying ointment or a solution to a parakeet. Here the sensitive cere of this small parrot is being treated.

1 **Holding the bird correctly.** This is the way to hold a bird when it needs to be treated. Hold it firmly enough to prevent the bird from struggling free, but do not press too hard.

3 **Liquid medication** is best administered with the aid of a pipette—according to precise instructions from the veterinarian.

degree that they die. In order to reveal the presence of this parasite, you need to cover the cage and nest box with a white cloth. At daybreak you can readily see the red parasites on the underside of the cloth.

During the day these mites hide in dark crevices, cracks in the wood, or in similar places. In this case, I also recommend that you consult a veterinarian, who will provide you with a suitable disinfecting agent.

Lice

These wingless insects live in the plumage of birds and feed on their feathers. They also reproduce among feathers, where they attach their eggs (nits) to feather branches. These lice (*Mallophages*) occur very rarely on parakeets that live indoors. They attack principally wild birds. Affected birds look rather tattered and torn. The parakeets scratch themselves more and more, because these pest organisms tend to cause itching. If you suspect these parasites have attacked your pets, it is best to consult a veterinarian immediately.

Skin Fungi

Skin fungi attack humans and animals and are not easy to treat. Fungi on parakeets often present a stubborn problem. The birds experience severe itching (puritus), which they try to relieve by scratching or pulling out feathers in the affected area. Some fungi species attack feathers, which causes a loss of uniform, shiny coloration. Do not hesitate to consult a veterinarian, because skin fungi can also be transmitted to

At the first sign of a disease in your parakeets, you must **consult a veterinarian** immediately. Parakeets are small birds that cannot withstand untreated diseases for long.

humans. Only the veterinarian is able to make a precise diagnosis, by means of a fungus culture.

Viral Diseases

I would like to mention only two virus diseases.

French Molt

In contrast to the regular molt, French Molt is a disease. Birds with this disease are referred to as runners or hoppers.
Symptoms: At an age of about four weeks, the parakeets will lose their just-matured primary and secondary flight feathers. They are no longer able to fly, and instead run around on the ground. Either the feathers will no longer regrow, or they keep falling out. Sometimes, birds with this affliction will grow feathers again when they are adults.

These two parakeets are healthy and happy.

Cause: *Polyoma* viruses. It is not known how these viruses are being transmitted.
Treatment: Treatment is not possible. A vaccine is under investigation, but not yet available. All you can do is to provide optimal care for the affected bird. Consult your veterinarian. Such birds should be accommodated in a separate, spacious cage with lots of natural branches for climbing. They should not be used for breeding purposes.

PBFD

This is an English initialism, meaning "psittacine beak and feather disease." This disease is highly contagious among parrots.
Symptoms: There is no clearly defined disease picture. After the outbreak of the disease there are growth disorders among the feathers. These can be pulled out easily and may exhibit color changes. From one molt to the next, these detrimental plumage changes become more profound. Even the horny areas on the beak and toes may start to change.
Cause: *Circo*-virus. The virus becomes established within the lymphatic system, in feather follicles, and in skin, as well as in the esophagus and in the crop.
Treatment: Unfortunately, treatment is not possible. For details talk to your veterinarian. Vaccines are being developed and tested, but there is no preventative vaccine on the market yet.

Inflammation of the Crop

Symptoms: By tossing their head, afflicted birds regurgitate discolored, brownish red mucus, which sticks to the head feathers. The crop inflammation is often accompanied by diarrhea.

Possible causes: There can be many reasons for the symptoms, such as plastic parts that may have been swallowed or consumption of a poisonous substance.

Treatment: Diagnosis and treatment should be done only by a veterinarian.

Transmission with *Chlamydia* is airborne contaminated dust particles.

Cause: *Chlamydia psittaci,* a type of bacteria.

Treatment: The veterinarian can determine the presence of these bacteria by means of a fecal examination. Nowadays there are excellent medications that promise successful treatment, so that afflicted parakeets—in contrast to earlier

DID YOU KNOW THAT . . .

. . . parakeet feathers are continuously replaced?

Wild parakeets do not have fixed molting periods. Their plumage is not replaced intermittently, but continuously throughout the year. The reason for that is simple: the birds must be able to fly at any time, in order to cover vast distances in their native country during periods of food shortages. In emergencies parakeets can even stop the molt altogether.

Parrot Disease (*Psittacosis*)

This disease is also known as *psittacosis, ornithosis,* and *clamydiosis.* The pathogen involved is transmissible to humans. If a bird has fallen ill from this disease, it must be reported to local health authorities.

Symptoms: Parakeets with this disease will hardly feed, have a fever, and suffer from diarrhea, severe respiratory distress, nasal catarrh, and purulent conjunctivitis. Humans with this disease initially display flu-like symptoms.

days—have excellent chances of survival and no longer need to be euthanized.

Going-light Syndrome (GLS)

GLS refers to a condition where birds are continuously losing weight in spite of eating normally. GLS is highly infectious for parrots. The entire flock in an aviary can be seriously endangered without anyone noticing anything unusual, because some birds carry the pathogen without exhibiting any disease symptoms. The pathogen is then excreted into the environment. That, of course, increases the risk of cross-infection to other birds.

Symptoms: In spite of increased food intake, there is a loss of body weight. The affected bird is regurgitating gray, glassy mucus and undigested seeds. Sometimes, blood and undigested seeds also appear in the feces.

Cause: *Macrorhabdos ornithogaster*, a yeast (*Saccaromycete*). This yeast prevents normal metabolic utilization of food. The effectiveness of the immune system is being reduced, especially that of the digestive track.

Treatment: For this disease, you must consult the veterinarian. So far, it has barely been researched and there is no effective therapy yet.

Note: Pay particular attention to hygiene. It is recommended that you acidify the drinking water slightly with ascorbic acid and apple-cider vinegar. You should feed very little of anything containing sugar because this withdraws the yeast's food supply.

Abscesses and Tumors

Swellings often occur in parakeets. When you feel or see swellings on your parakeet, such as on the chest region, do not go into a panic, because many tumors and abscesses are harmless and not malignant.

Symptoms: *Lipomas*, spherical fatty tumors, can often be found in the chest region. They impede the bird's flying capability or affect its movement. Some lipomas can weigh up to $\frac{1}{3}$ ounce (10 g), an unbelievable weight, considering the total weight of a parakeet is only 1.5 ounce (50 g).

Cause: This is often unclear and usually has nothing to do with the care and maintenance regimen.

Treatment: Diagnosis and a recommendation for treatment can be made only by a veterinarian, who will usually recommend surgical removal under anesthesia.

This Is What You Can Do

Diarrhea: Normal feces harden within a few minutes, and can then easily be removed from any substrate. If the consistency and color of feces changes, or the frequency of defecation, and if the cloacal region is dirty, special attention is required. Diarrhea can have many different causes. If it continues for several days, you should visit the

◀ *A box made of plastic can be useful for a gentle transport to the veterinarian, and it is easy to clean.*

veterinarian who will examine the feces in the laboratory.

Nasal secretion: The sneezing of a parakeet is barely audible. If the bird sneezes frequently and has a nasal discharge, caution is advised. In the simplest case, this is merely a reaction to the ambient climate. Air that is too dry often causes sneezing. If, however, this is the onset of a cold, the veterinarian should be consulted. Make sure the bird lives in an even-temperature environment and is protected against drafts.

Administering Medication

When administering medication it is very important to comply with the dosage recommendation and with the necessary treatment duration. Do not play "doctor" with your parakeet. Treatment mistakes can have fatal consequences for the little bird.

If a medication is to be administered via drinking water, the bird must not be able to quench its thirst at some other location. If it is given via the food, the food bowl should never be filled to the brim, since this clever little parakeet can toss the medication out of the bowl with its beak. Some medications have to be given via the beak. For that, you have to handle the bird as shown in the photo on page 89. Hold the bird slightly on its back and drip the required amount through the side of the beak onto the tongue. For this a disposable syringe without needle is often very helpful. Make sure that the medication does not go down the wrong way and enter the trachea (windpipe). However, if the bird keeps the beak tightly closed, it becomes difficult. Try to insert your fingernail—cautiously—between the

CHECKLIST

First Aid Kit for Parakeets

It is fundamentally important and very useful to have a few items always on hand for administering first aid in case your parakeets become sick or injured.

- ○ Infrared heat lamp (see page 88)

- ○ Hemostatic cotton (or suitable alternative like cotton gauze or cotton balls)

- ○ Vitamin and calcium preparation for the molt

- ○ Disposable syringes (without needles)

- ○ Cotton swabs, for applying ointments, etc.

- ○ Small wooden spatula or popsicle stick that the bird can take into its beak during treatment

- ○ Sterile sodium chloride solution for washing out wounds, etc.

upper and lower beak and gently force open the beak. Admittedly, this is a difficult undertaking, and it may be advisable to ask your veterinarian to show you the procedure.

Note: If the sick parakeet shares the cage with another one, you have to ask the veterinarian whether the healthy bird can also use the medicated drinking water or food without sustaining any harm. If not, you have to separate the two birds. Make sure they can see and hear each other. That is important for the psyche of the sick parakeet and has beneficial, healing effects.

Questions:
All About Parakeet Care and Health

When I take Pauli in my hand to cut his claws, the bird screeches loudly and I can feel his heart beating. What is the best way to relieve his stress? First, to prevent Pauli's stress you should provide him with natural branches of different diameters. Taking a parakeet into your hand should be done only in extreme emergencies, such as treating a particular disease, or for essential procedures, such as trimming the claws. Parakeets are extremely scared of human hands and will defend themselves with biting. Therefore, I offer this advice: Wear protective gloves when you physically handle your parakeet. You can also use a small soft cloth, such as a bath cloth if gloves seem to frighten your bird. By far the safest way to take hold of your parakeet is to darken the room, with the birds still in the cage. Wait for 10 to 15 minutes before gently reaching for the bird. The parakeet will have adjusted to the darkness and will not see your hand approaching. Do not hold the bird too tightly, but make your grip sufficiently secure so that it cannot escape. The ideal position is to have the bird with its back in the palm of your hand, and your index finger and thumb around the neck, so that the head protrudes freely (see page 89).

We will spend our three-week vacation in an Italian vacation home. Are there any problems with taking my two parakeets with me? It is best to leave the birds at home. The transport and the unusual noises will be too stressful for them. Moreover, most countries do not permit the import and export of parakeets (without official documentation). Therefore, it is best to find someone who will look after the birds and will give them some free-flight time. This is the easiest way for the birds to handle the separation. Beyond that, if the parakeet has a mate, the two of them are less likely to get bored. It would be ideal if the sitter knows your birds already. This way, the birds do not have to get used to a stranger. There is, of course, also the possibility of approaching your veterinarian, pet shop, or animal protection organization for the name and address of an animal sitter or someone who will board the birds for a nominal fee. Another avenue is to make appropriate inquiries via the Internet. Provide explicit instructions for the animal sitter about the expected care of your parakeets (see Pet Sitter Checklist, page 136). In any event, leave your vacation address and telephone number with your veterinarian.

Recently, Punky stopped preening himself. What does that mean? A parakeet that neglects plumage grooming

is sick. Do not delay taking your bird immediately to the veterinarian. Birds as small as parakeets can die quickly once they have become sick.

I believe that the cage should be disinfected at regular intervals. What is your opinion? A preventive, regular disinfection of the cage is—within a normal hygienic maintenance program—especially necessary if your parakeets suffer from a transmissible disease, or parasites have become established. In such a case, ask your veterinarian for a suitable disinfectant. Prior to disinfection, you must take the parakeets out of their cage. Under no circumstances must your birds be exposed to commercial disinfectant sprays. If some of the spray gets into a bird's nose, beak, or eyes, it can have serious health consequences for the bird.

What do I do if one of my parakeets is accidentally injured during free flight? If you have removed all potential danger sources, the chance of being injured during free flight should be minimal. Nevertheless, if an accident does happen, approach the bird without panicking. Bleeding wounds should be covered with clean gauze or cotton cloth and apply light pressure. Using extreme caution, transfer the bird into a transport cage, where the bottom has been padded with soft paper (e.g., kitchen paper towel). Proceed immediately to a veterinarian.

I have often heard the term egg binding concerning female parakeets. Could you please explain to me what is meant by that term? Egg binding refers to difficulties encountered by a female during the process of laying eggs. In such a case, the female is unable to push an egg out of the oviduct and cloaca. Suspicion of egg binding is indicated when a female acts lethargically, gives off unusually large fecal balls, and frequently whips her tail up and down while pushing heavily. This diagnosis becomes even clearer when you take the bird into your hand and gently stroke your fingers over the abdomen. When you do that, you may feel an egg. I strongly urge against any home treatment. Without sufficient experience, it is not easy to remove such an egg. An experienced veterinarian is better at that task. See your veterinarian immediately once you notice signs of egg binding. If you do not do that, you are exposing the female to unnecessary, life-threatening danger.

Activities
and Learning

Parakeets as pets have a lot of spare time. For your little parrots to remain physically and mentally fit, they need a comprehensive learning and activity program.

Special Training for Parakeets

Boredom is unhealthy—for us as well as for our pets. Although a second parakeet in the same cage can help pass the time, that alone is not sufficient. Instead, you should help by placing physical and intellectual demands on your parakeets.

Scientifically there is no doubt: Animals with a large brain (relative to their body mass) are among the most intelligent individuals. This body mass to brain ratio is easy to understand, when we look at elephants. These animals certainly have a much larger brain than humans do, but they also weigh between 5 and 7 tons. Yet, when one transposes that fact to the size of their brain, elephants have a small brain. Humans belong to those living beings with the largest brain. This is also true for birds. Ravens and parrots have brains nearly equal in size to those of the most intelligent mammals, the chimpanzees.

Learn for Life While Playing

What does the size of a brain have to do with playing? Intelligent animals love to play a lot, because they do not view the world with a completed instinct program. Only through playing and learning do they experience the world around them. Parakeets also belong to the "players." Their brain is also very large relative to their body mass. However, among intelligent living beings, playing is everything but a form of

killing time; it also has an important biological purpose. While playing, birds are training safely for fitness and coordination, experimenting with types of behavior, and developing strategies for real-life situations. For young animals, play is a particularly important investment in their future. The most compulsive players among the birds are—by a substantial margin—large parrots (especially keas) and ravenlike birds. Adult parakeets do not seem to play in nature; at least there are no written accounts of it. Apparently, there is no time for this in their daily fight for

Parakeets are ▶
extremely curious.
Everything is being
investigated and
nibbled on with
the beak.

survival. However, they have a lot of time in the care of humans. Therefore, playing and learning are the absolute highlights in their life as pets. With that in mind, you should offer your little parrots diverse toys.

Always something to do

▶ 1 **Uncooked pasta** provides a harmless pastime. Noodles are investigated with the beak, pushed back and forth, and sometimes even carried into the cage.

▶ 2 **Non-toxic paint** in various circles in different colors onto a white sheet of paper fascinates parakeets. Birds can even be allowed to pick up nontoxic colored pencils in their beaks.

Games that Provide Fun and Stimulate Thinking

Adult parakeets rarely play with each other as such. They are usually only interested in one particular toy, with which they play with amazing endurance. However, parakeets will play only in a relaxed environment. They must feel contented and must not be afraid. Music that is too loud and consists of high notes, slamming doors, or rattling dishes impedes playing.

Large marbles: Parakeets can keep themselves busy for hours with glass marbles, by letting them collide with each other. The birds become excited by their rolling around and the sounds they create.

Water ball: A grape is particularly suited as a ball when floating in a small, water-filled plastic bowl. The water level must not be more than 1¼ inch (3 cm) maximum. Courageous birds will climb immediately into the water and play with the fruit. Those birds that are more reluctant will try every trick in the book to reach the floating object from the safe ground outside the bowl. Make sure to supervise this activity—birds can drown in small amounts of water.

Lattice ball: Ball games are always popular. A lattice ball is ideal for rolling around in the palm of the trusted human's hand; it can be picked up with the beak and then dropped again.

Bells: Simply suspend the little bell in the climbing tree and attach a string to the tongue of the bell. I can virtually assure you that your parakeet is a born bell ringer. Make sure the bird can't remove the clapper.

Swing: It is understood that a swing is part of the basic furnishings of a birdcage. Pet shops offer numerous varieties of swings. However, just as much fun as a swing is a natural branch suspended at either end by a string from the cage or aviary ceiling.

Pencil game: While you are writing a note, particularly confident parakeets will fly onto your hand and nibble on the pencil. If you stretch out your arm (with the back of the hand pointing upward) and move it quickly from side to side, the little parrot will briefly fly up and down again. The bird enjoys the speed. If it could, it would scream with joy!

Adventure Playground

So that your parakeets can satisfy their innate playing behavior, you should build them an adventure playground. The advantage is that your home furnishings, wallpaper, and so on will be protected against unsightly gnawing marks, because the little birds investigate everything with their beaks. Two climbing trees connected by ropes would be ideal. Climbing trees made out of natural branches are commercially available from pet shops. However, you can also make one yourself. Take a heavy piece of untreated timber $^3/_4$ to $1^1/_4$ inch (2 to 3 cm) thick, with an area of 12 by 12 inches (30 × 30 cm), drill a hole into the middle of the timber, and screw in a thick branch $1^1/_4$ to $1^1/_2$ inches (3 to 4 cm) diameter with lots of smaller branches, and there you have your climbing tree. The size of the piece of timber that makes up the platform is of course dependent upon the size of the branch. Make sure that the structure is stable and does not fall over with the first flying approach by the birds.

Connect the climbing trees with a climbing rope made of natural fibers (such as bast) that contains a few knots over the length of the rope. You could secure some spray millet in these knots. The parakeets enjoy pulling, tugging, and nibbling on the natural-colored fiber ropes. Now the climbing tree will be decorated like a Christmas tree.

Activity makes life **worthwhile.** Offer your parakeets sufficient diversity.

A swing with the bell will be the highlight. Like acrobats, the birds will climb around the "tree" and onto the swing (available from pet shops) and ring the bell.

A fruit or vegetable skewer ensures the retention of a slim physique and is a lot of fun. Push fruit and vegetable pieces in an alternating pattern onto a metal skewer, and suspend it from the tree. Climbing balls can also be suspended in the tree. These are just a few suggestions. There are no limits to your imagination. However, it is important that these trees be "redecorated" periodically, or at least that the objects be moved around; otherwise the playground gets boring.

Parakeets Must Never Be Bored

Life in nature cannot be compared to life under human care. Out there in the wild, the harsh laws of nature dictate the daily fight for survival: Searching for food and water, avoiding predators, the climate, and selecting a partner and rearing young are just a few examples. Every day, new problems have to be solved, and any bird that fails is in mortal danger. Parakeets are well equipped for their fight for survival and their intelligence helps them with it. They do not have any enemies while in human care, and there is no need for the perpetual search for food. Birds that have a partner can handle the situation much better. They can communicate and express their feelings toward each other. However, in my opinion that is far from being sufficient to fill out the "free time" the birds have when we look after them.

The activity can be of different types: free flying in the room, looking for hidden food, and resolving "thinking tasks." The indoor free flight has essentially two objectives: It serves both body and mind. Therefore it is essential that the birds learn to use the room (see page 46). Newly acquired parakeets often seem uninterested in flying and prefer to remain inside the secure cage. Make freedom attractive for the bird. This is best achieved with some spray

millet placed at the open cage door. If the desire for a tasty treat wins, you will have succeeded. With that, the little bird will have realized that nothing bad happens to it outside the cage. With a full stomach, the bird flies the first few rounds, followed by rest periods on top of a bureau or the curtain rods. The strange new world is easier to explore when you have a partner; one gives the other courage. If the bird does not yet return to the cage on its own, a piece of spray millet at the cage door will again prove to be helpful. Never try to catch the bird with your hands! Even if you can catch the bird, the stress involved will lead to a deep-seated scare, and it will take a long time to recover the lost trust (see page 63).

Parakeets Enjoy Learning

These birds not only like to learn, but also learn incredibly fast. Some can actually dazzle an audience as much as circus performers with their amazing performances. They can pull small wagons, climb at great speed, or, if desired, make a precision landing. So much ability and acrobatic talent presupposes daily instructions from an experienced trainer. Presumably, you do not have the time for comprehensive training, but with a degree of intuition and some patience, you can induce your birds to perform remarkable feats. Unfortunately, many parakeet owners do not take advantage of this, because they are unaware of the significance of learning for the well-being of their little birds. The genes of parakeets decree that they must learn. That is the plan of nature, or to put it more scientifically, they have at their disposal certain learn-

Sacrifice an old book for the birds and they will shred it to pieces with great enthusiasm.
▼

ing dispositions. Without the ability to learn, they would succumb in nature. Learning permits them to quickly adapt to environmental changes. This way they become fit to withstand the daily challenges.

A parakeet that wants to survive in the barren outback of the Australian continent needs to know the location of the nearest watering hole, whether it carries water or whether it has dried up. The bird learns early which plants (or seeds) it can eat, which enemies are

Establish Appropriate Preconditions

Parakeets need a relaxed environment. Therefore, you should work with your birds only when there are no loud, screeching noises in the vicinity. These will scare the birds and cause them to fly away. Punishing the birds is forbidden; only rewards will succeed. Food is usually the best stimulus. Solving the tasks must be pure play. The birds are

DID YOU KNOW THAT . . .

. . . every parakeet has a distinctive personality?

One parakeet is not like any other parakeet. You will notice that yourself, when you are keeping more than one bird. One may be shy, whereas the other is adventurous. The next one is a bit "talkative," while the next one is quieter. There are little "Einsteins" that have a quick solution for everything, and those who need more time to solve a problem.

waiting for it, and how to escape them. The list of what a parakeet in the wild has to learn goes on and on. But that is not the intent and purpose of this pet guide; that information is included only to demonstrate how pitiful life is for an individual parakeet that has to linger on in his cage day after day without being permitted to learn anything. Admittedly, it is difficult to imagine what stimuli and activities such a small bird needs. Yet I am convinced that it is not much less than what must be provided to a dog.

more attentive when given "private" instructions. Having other birds around tends to distract them. Young parakeets learn very quickly, but even older birds are still open for new tasks. About two to three weeks after leaving the nest, young parakeets will explore their surroundings intensively (see page 123). That is a good opportunity to start the first training sessions. The birds learn more easily and quickly in their familiar surroundings. There they feel secure and are not distracted by other sensory perceptions.

and gradually increase the flight distance. After a little while, the parakeet will fly to you as soon as you have called out its name. Once hand tamed, parakeets can be enrolled in "bird school." When a parakeet has learned a particular exercise, it automatically becomes the teacher for its feathered friends. Help to start out is no longer required from the human owner, because the entire flock learns through observations.

Things Parakeets Learn Easily

These small parrots have an excellent spatial memory. They learn very quickly where something is hidden. You can easily check that.

Searching for food: Hide three identical food bowls at different locations in the room that can be readily approached by flying parakeets. For the first trial, place some millet spikes into all three bowls. As expected, the bird encounters one of these food bowls purely by coincidence on one of its exploratory tours through the room. After it has fed, the bird will try its luck at the second and the third bowls, feeding on the seeds provided. After one or two flying approaches, the bird knows that a treat is hidden in the bowls, and after that, it flies directly to the bowls. Now the actual experiment starts: place food as a reward into only one of the bowls. As soon as the bird has figured it out, it will always fly first to that particular bowl.

What can be achieved with praise and reprimand in dogs does not work with birds. Parakeets have to be virtually enticed to learn. That can be achieved only by attracting their attention and awakening their curiosity. For example, in a flight lesson, the bird is to fly to you. This exercise sounds simple enough, but it requires a lot of sensitivity on your part. Train only one bird at a time; otherwise the distraction is too large. Position yourself with a treat (maybe a spike of millet) at a distance of about 6½ feet (2 m) from the parakeet. Call its name softly, or click your tongue to arouse its curiosity. As soon as the bird has focused in on you, gradually approach the bird, holding the millet spike horizontally in front of your body.

The bird will not be able to resist for long and will land on the tempting treat. Repeat this exercise several times

If you are interested, you can make the task more difficult by letting the parakeet select between two food bowls. The old bowl remains the same; the new one is distinctly marked with a black spot. Both of these bowls are placed side-by-side within 3 feet (1 m) distance of each other, so that the bird can easily look into the bowls. Food is only in the marked bowl. Now the bird will require slightly longer because it has to recognize and then memorize that the food is only in the marked bowl.

Recognizing colors: Because I like to give my parakeets learning tasks and puzzles to solve, for which they have to work out a solution for themselves, I have built a sort of "experiment table." For that, I have used a board 4-feet (1.2-m) long and 10-inches (25-cm) wide, with slight depressions drilled out (much like a painter's palette), into which I can fit the sleeve of small (tea light) candles. Be careful not to let your bird nibble on the wax and ingest it while practicing this training exercise. The edge of the tea light protrudes above the shallow depression. I have arranged these depressions in the shape of a cross (three horizontal depressions, and two vertical ones, whereby the central horizontal ones form the intersection). This way I can train the birds to recognize many different constellations or colors. You can paint the tea candles in different colors, and so test whether your parakeets can discriminate between colors. Place the board onto a stool or a chair. Paint one of the tea candle sleeves green, the other red, and

2 **Reading** is not yet a skill these two have, but it looks like they want to learn that. However, no doubt it is more likely the paper they are interested in, because it can be turned into such beautiful confetti.

▼

▲

1 **Lid test.** Encourage your parakeet to solve little problems. Here are some small food bowls covered by lids. Which bird finds out quickest how to get at the food?

place a red and green lid on them respectively. Some birds are unable to lift the lid. Show the bird by pushing the lid away with your finger. Now place food in the green container and leave the red one empty. The parakeet will learn quickly where the food is. To make sure that it has memorized the color and not the location, place the container at a different place on the board. You will notice that the bird flies to the green one. Using this method, you can test all colors with the bird. You can also check whether it can distinguish shapes. For that, you can use candle containers that are painted and cover them with a lid onto which the respective shapes have been painted conspicuously. One of my very tame parakeets had a lot of fun annoying the children in their "catch the hat" game. Purzel, a male, would nibble on the hats until one fell over. Clearly, at the beginning this was not intentional, but it really shows how capable these little parrots are of learning things. Immediately afterward Purzel would topple the hats purposely, much to the annoyance of the children. Whenever they were playing the game, Purzel flew and toppled the hats.

TOYS PREFERRED BY PARAKEETS

THIS IS HOW THEY REMAIN FIT

Swing	A swing develops a sense of balance and assures physical fitness.
Lattice ball	Rolling the ball around promotes alertness. The birds like to take it into their beaks and toss it around.
Climbing rope	A climbing rope with thick knots promotes precise landing and invites climbing or swinging.
Paper balls	Balls are examined in detail with the beak, and are kicked about. Rustling paper stimulates curiosity even more.
Natural fiber threads (bast)	Tie 6-inch (15-m) long, natural bast threads together in the middle with another thread. Suspend the bundle inside the cage. The birds will pull on the individual threads with dedication. This enhances their manipulative skills.
Uncooked pasta	Pasta can be pushed around on a plate using the beak; it also makes interesting rattling sounds.

Misjudged Geniuses

Discoveries in the area of bird intelligence are becoming more and more amazing. It appears that even in the small parakeet there is much more than we have ever expected. Consequently, it is even more important to offer these little birds an interesting life as pets.

Does a parakeet actually know who its human partner is? Expressed differently, does the bird recognize you as a particular individual? Does the bird know that it is you and not your partner or a child? Much suggests that it is so. A random event sparked this question in me.

"Masked Ball" in the Parakeet Aviary

One day I entered my aviary with a cap on my head and my parakeets became terribly frightened. They fluttered about wildly, although I had entered the aviary the same as always, softly whistling and talking to them. This is the way I always announced my visit. It is a sort of "knocking on the door" to prepare the little parrots for my arrival. However, this time there was this excited reaction. What did it mean? I wanted to find out what had happened, so I conducted some pilot tests. These were not precise scientific experiments, but perhaps they would reveal a trend. I changed my appearance in the head region. In one trial I wore a peaked cap, then a false nose with a headphone, then a headband and a pair of sunglasses, then a headband with feathers, and then the false nose only. The reactions of the

parakeets in response to the different masks were variable. The false nose and head band with feathers upset them the least. On the other hand, the cap on my head elicited the strongest reaction. None of the birds flew directly onto my hand, which was the usual thing for them to do. Obviously, they did not recognize me in my costumes. Professor Fritz Trillmich did not investigate whether parakeets recognize people individually, but whether parakeets recognize each other individually. However, his results are still very revealing. Parakeets recognize each other optically, specifically in the head region. With skillful selection trials, Trillmich was able to document this scientifically. The birds recognize themselves even on color slides. During that experiment, he showed slides of known and unknown parakeets to the birds. The birds chose their known partners.

Sounds also play an important role for individual recognition in the wild. Nevertheless, the image is already sufficient to find out who is who. It is incredible what our little parrots can do. However, that also places an obligation on us. We should not give our birds to just anybody or anyplace—even if only for a few vacation days. This is particularly stressful for single parakeets. That bird knows you and is dependent on you.

A Surprisingly Good Memory

Anyone with a good memory finds learning easier. The ability of parakeets to memorize is simply astonishing. I myself have seen a bird immediately recognize its former owner and warble his favorite song after a separation of four years! That is not an individual case! Unfortunately, a scientific analysis of parakeet memory is—to my knowledge—still outstanding. I cannot understand that, because it is so easy to talk to such eloquent little students.

Brainy "Heads"

We can only be in awe at the amazing capabilities of birds. They fly thousands of miles to reach their breeding and feeding grounds, and they breed in the Antarctic at 30° below the freezing point. Some, like hummingbirds, can virtually "stand still" in midair to lick nectar from flowers. Others are skilled divers and fish eaters. Parakeets fly hundreds of miles to follow rain and then breed there. So far, nobody knows how these birds perceive the rain. In fact, birds are among the most intelligent animals. It is generally known that our closest relative, the chimpanzee, takes first place in a ranking on intelligence. Its principal competition comes from ravens, crows, magpies, keas, and gray parrots.

Mirror test: I had a friend who referred to his magpies as "feathered chimpanzees," and for good reason. His magpie Gerti recognized herself in a mirror. Only a few animal species—presumably only six—are capable of doing that. The mirror test provides information about whether animals have self-awareness. It is the probe to the consciousness of animals. Dogs and cats do not pass the test, and children only from the age of about two years onward.

"Toolmaker": The scientific world was also amazed by Betty, a New Caledonian crow. On the occasion of a visit to Oxford, England I had the opportunity to visit that crow. The bird was able to bend a copper wire so that a hook was formed at the end. Nobody had shown the bird how to do it, much less trained her for this task. With this "tool," the bird would "fish" in a food bowl (that had an attached handle) from a large

◀ *A thick rope, a few cereal spikes, and some colorful wooden beads become a gently swinging adventure playground. That will make a parakeet's heart beat faster.*

container. However, that is not a special case; the bird's siblings in the wild are similarly clever. These birds can produce and use tools and—this is the decisive point—they can also modify a tool to fit a particular function, very much like we adjust a skeleton key to pick a lock. Betty's abilities were a scientific sensation; to that point, such capabilities had been known only from primitive man—the start of technology.

New Findings About the Brain

Why did we not expect such intelligence from birds? Because of the structure of their brains. The brains of mammals and birds consists of various components. Mammals as well as birds have the same brain areas, but these are differently developed in the two groups. For instance, that part of the brain with which we or, for example, chimpanzees, think (the cerebrum) is smaller in birds. Other brain areas that have little to do with our thinking processes are larger in birds. The conclusion was that birds are less able to think, but instead are guided more by instincts. But modern research using the latest technologies revealed that in birds other parts of the brain also facilitate thinking. This knowledge placed birds in a new light for us. Yet, what are all these generalities about the intelligence of birds doing in a guide on parakeets? For me, as one who has studied parakeets for more than 30 years, the answer is easy. The mental capacities of this little parrot have been underestimated. I am certain that there are still some surprises waiting for us in the near future. Of course, parakeets are not like gray parrots or ravens; however, they too have . . . . "brainy heads."

CHECKLIST

Learning per a Study Program

Parakeets require a lot of activity. However, for a structured learning program for these birds, you need to accept a few rules.

○ **Hours of instruction.** Start the training exercises only when your parakeet is wide awake and alert. That is usually in the morning and in the evening, and always when the bird is curiously exploring the world around it.

○ **Individual training sessions.** The bird will find it easier to learn without other birds around when it is concentrating on you.

○ **Brief training sessions.** Short instructional units of 10 minutes at the most are more productive than an entire "school hour." The attention span in all animals declines rapidly.

○ **Volunteers only.** Never exert force on your feathered friend or ask for too much; otherwise, the bird is no longer interested.

○ **Motivation.** It is difficult to study on a full stomach. When slightly hungry, the bird learns more quickly and can be motivated by tasty treats.

○ **Soft and gentle.** During the training session, you should speak with a soft voice to the bird and avoid all hectic movements.

Small Acrobats

▶ **1** **Climbing** cannot be avoided when one wants to reach tasty leaves and flowers. However, the branches are rather thin and are shaking enormously.

▶ **2** **Skillful gymnastics** are easy for parakeets. If need be, the beak can be used for holding on.

▶ **3** A "split" on the "vertical bar" is hard for anyone to follow.

Talented "Talkers"

There are distinct speech geniuses among parakeets, which have been found to mimic more than 300 simple sentences, 500 words, and 8 children's songs. Vocalization in parakeets has been the focus of research for years. The results are also of importance for bird hobbyists, because they show how important a partner is. Parakeets belong to those few birds that learn new sounds throughout their lifespan, especially males, because in the competition for females, talent for sound mimicry is of profound importance. In fact, males are able to persuade a female by imitating her song. The female will prefer the male that is best at it, and the other ones will miss out. In essence, then, females judge courting males by how well they have learned the new song. The learning ability of males in respect to their song is being screened by a stringent selection procedure. The other way around, nothing happens. Females do not imitate males. Consequently, it is not surprising, when males in particular are mimicking human speech. Yet, females are not exactly mute, as everybody knows. Their talkativeness is less involved during the courtship, but more so in the daily lives of parakeets.

Flock cohesion is ensured by contact calls, among other things. That conforms largely to my own observations, when a new bird is introduced into my aviary. At the beginning, the others look upon the new one cautiously and it takes some time until the new bird is fully accepted. Now we know why: The new bird must first learn the dialect. This is not much different from humans when we travel to foreign lands. As much as the appearance of parakeets has been changed through captive breeding, they have fortunately retained their ability to learn new sounds. This was demonstrated by studies made by Susan M. Farabaugh. She compared the sound repertoire of wild-caught parakeets with those from among our domesticated birds, and

did not find any differences. I sincerely hope that after having read these explanations, every bird keeper understands how terrible it must be for a parakeet when it cannot hear other parakeets nearby and must live alone.

The Art of Imitation

Imitating is the forte of these little parrots, but not only in respect to singing. Once a bird knows, for example, how to push a toy car, one can bet that the other birds will quickly do the same. In the wild, parakeets often ensure their survival through observing and imitating, and so avoid dangerous, individual experiments. Cecilia Heyes and Anna Saggerson were able to underpin the observational ability of parakeets in an elegant experiment. The candidates were young female and male parakeets. The task involved for these birds was to watch how another parakeet would get at the food. To do that, the birds had to remove two differently colored obstacles

in order to expose a slot in the lid. This way the bird could get to the desired food source.

The obstacles could be removed only by pushing them with the beak or pulling them away. It took quite a while for the first test candidates to reach the target and receive the food reward after several fruitless attempts. The other parakeets that observed this undertaking were significantly more focused and

TIP

"Speech" lessons

Practice with individual birds. Start out by saying only a single word, something like *good* or *beautiful*, repeatedly. The first time the bird replies with the same sound, it is given a treat. After the lesson, the parakeet is returned to its bird partner in the cage.

MY PET

How to improve your parakeets' intelligence

You will be surprised at the intelligent activities your little parrots are capable of doing. This particular test does not involve learning, but the solving of a problem. The secret of the lid is a tricky one.

The test starts:

Take a food bowl and cover it with a cardboard lid. The bird is sitting on your hand and can easily see you placing a treat into the bowl and covering it up with the lid. Next, repeat the same with a transparent, lightweight plastic lid and let the bird solve the problem. Do this test shortly before the regular feeding time, so that the bird is slightly hungry.

My test results:

solved the given task almost immediately. Therefore, parakeets are able to imitate not only sounds but also complex actions (sequences). Yet, the art of imitating is not as easy as first thought. Imitating presupposes that one perceives what the other is doing and then translates that action into one's own action.

Creative Thinking

Susie, my five-year-old female parakeet, was no longer able to fly because she had a broken wing. Nevertheless, that did not impede her curiosity. She was only able to fly down—which she frequently did—to discover everything

that was there to discover. In spite of this handicap, the bird did not have any difficulty during her excursions until she attempted to return to the cage, which was on a cabinet. I positioned an old cage in front of the cabinet, in effect providing climbing scaffolding. However, what I observed was indeed exciting. By coincidence, the door of the support cage was open so that Susie could simply walk in. Yet, she did not climb up on the inside walls only to discover that access to her regular cage was blocked off; instead she did something very different. Susie remained at the bottom, looked obliquely upward, walked a few times back and forth, and then looked obliquely up again.

Determined, she then marched out of the support cage and climbed along the outside back into the regular cage. She discovered the return passage, not by trial and error, but by . . . thinking. Thinking means to first assess a situation in your head, and then to test the reality by your own action. Admittedly, it could have been a coincidence, but this is contradicted by the fact that on the next day the bird climbed up the outside of the cage without hesitation. She had learned her lesson.

Scientists at a university in Germany approached parakeet intelligence in the following way: They wanted to know whether parakeets are able to transfer the principles of a task once learned to another, similar task. The birds had learned to push up a little door after three blocking bolts along the left side of the door had been pulled out of their respective, drilled holes. When the wooden bolts were on the right side instead of the left, the birds would still try their luck for short while on the left side (site fixation). However, as soon as they observed the change of side, the birds figured it out. They pulled out the bolts on the right side. In fact, they also did it when the number of bolts was increased and similarly, when the shape and color of the bolts were changed. They comprehended the principle.

Independent of the number of bolts used, and irrespective of what color, what shape, and at what location, the birds needed to understand: *In order to push the little door upwards I must first remove the bolts.* Our parakeets are indeed quite clever.

The young, enthusiastic parakeet hobbyist Sandra Weidenmüller investigated the problem solving behavior of parakeets. Among other things, she suspended a piece of spray millet from a string and attached it to a perch. Two of her seven birds pulled up the millet with their beak. The others attempted to fly at the millet or climb downward along the string. Her experiment is documented in the photograph shown on page 45.

Even the ripe sunflower provides diversity; moreover, the seeds taste very good.

▼

New Arrivals in the
Parakeet Home

It is very touching to experience the tender courtship rituals
of a parakeet pair and their loving care when raising their chicks.
However, are you able to guarantee the young birds a good life?

"Family Planning" for Parakeets

The nest box is suspended at the right place, and the future parent pair understand each other perfectly. Soon the desire for progeny will be fulfilled. That will be a difficult time for male and female, because from the onset the young parakeets require constant attention.

Parakeets make a particularly delightful loving couple that cares for its young with great dedication. Anyone who has seen the pair billing and preening each other, and how the male feeds the female, is unlikely to refuse their desire for offspring. However, before you commit yourself to such an exciting adventure, there are few things to plan and to consider.

What to Do With the Progeny?

Do not give parakeets away to be kept as individual birds. The new owner must be aware that parakeets can reach an age of up to 15 years. That will scare off many people. Investigate closely whether the new owner handles parakeets responsibly and does not simply lock them up in a cage when it becomes too cumbersome to provide adequate free-flight time for the birds. Unfortunately, that occurs more frequently than you can imagine. Only when I have first convinced myself about the husbandry conditions provided do I give my juvenile parakeets to new owners.

Healthy Parents

Select only healthy birds as breeding stock. They must not have any physical deficiencies, such as crippled feet and inadequate plumage. If you are buying an additional bird specifically for breeding purposes, you should get a young one, since older birds could possibly be no longer suitable for breeding because of certain experiences earlier in their lives. Some parakeets have become too imprinted on humans and therefore have difficulties in pair formation.

A young parakeet is being fed inside the nest box. However, it will not be long before the young bird is fully fledged.

Although parakeets reach sexual maturity within a few months, I do not let my birds breed until they are about one year old. At that age, the birds are fully grown and strong enough to withstand the strains of raising a brood. This is also beneficial for the young. Do not use physically large and heavy parakeets for breeding. Such birds are in a less than perfect condition than those with

they are siblings. The danger is much too large that such inbreeding can reveal masked diseases.

Basic Building Blocks of Genetics

The characteristics of all living beings are embedded in their hereditary material. What we become and what we are is largely keyed in our DNA. This is the hereditary molecule of living beings.

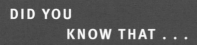

DID YOU
KNOW THAT . . .

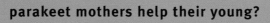

parakeet mothers help their young?

If a chick is too weak to free itself from the eggshell, the parakeet mother—in contrast to most other bird species—will help her child. She nibbles at the eggshell until the chick has been freed. With such a rescue strategy for emergencies that threaten the unborn, female parakeets even out life-threatening climatic influences in their native country.

a normal weight. Moreover, they lay fewer eggs. Large females produce large eggs and therefore require more calcium for the formation of eggshells. The increased demand for calcium can be a limiting factor for healthy growth. Selective breeding for particular characteristics (such as size and weight), often has disadvantages for the body since these characteristics are usually genetically controlled.

Note: Irrespective of how tenderly your parakeet pair treat each other, I strongly advise against breeding such birds if

DNA: The information of the DNA can be compared to a computer program. The fact that our hand has five fingers is stored in our DNA. Rarely are there people with six fingers. If there are, the DNA has been modified accordingly. This can be compared to a writing program. For instance, changing the word *house* to the word *louse* or to the word *mouse* may involve only a single lowercase letter, but it leads to a major change. Many diseases in humans and animals have originated that way and will continue to do so.

Before you start breeding parakeets, you will need to think about the **future of the young**. Will you be able to find people who are going to provide loving care and attention to the young birds, or are you going to keep them for yourself?

Traits and characteristics: How are these being inherited? In all higher living beings, the hereditary information is stored in cells and their nuclei. The storage location for the gene (hereditary factors)are the chromosomes. These are comparable to strings that contain *quipu* (or *khipu*), sometimes also called "talking knots." Father and mother always have a duplicate number of chromosomes, except in egg cells and sperm. There we always find half of the chromosome numbers. My cells possess 46 chromosomes and so do yours. Each parent contributes only half, i.e., 23 chromosomes, to their children. The new organism again has 46 chromosomes, where father and mother each contribute half of them. However, not all genes are equal. Some are dominant over others. These are referred to as dominant genes, which then manifest themselves by visible traits in the organism. Submissive genes are referred to as being recessive. These become visible only in an individual when they are present in duplicate or the dominant gene is not present. This is the same in parakeets. Blue parakeets, for instance, occur because father and mother have passed on the same gene for the color blue. We assigned the letter *f* to the gene for the color blue. The lowercase letter means recessive. A blue parakeet, therefore, has in its hereditary material the lowercase *f* and is pure (homozygous).

If, however, the parents pass on different genes, e.g. the father *F* and the mother *f*, the offspring are heterozygous. They have an uppercase *F* and a lowercase *f* in their hereditary material. The uppercase letter means that the gene is dominant. The gene for the color green is dominant and receives the letter *F*. The progeny are also all green. Geneticists have a simpler way of writing this: father (FF) × mother (ff); since male as well as female pass on only one *F* or *f* each to a child, the children are always (Ff), that is, heterozygous and green. Green parakeets can carry different genes. They can be pure (homozygous) with both genes (FF)

Only healthy birds should be used for breeding. ▶

and heterozygous with both genes (Ff). Blue parakeets are always pure and always carry two recessive genes (ff). With the progeny from two heterozygous green parakeets, it can happen that blue parakeets are born. In that case, the mother has transferred her gene (f) and the father his gene (f) to the progeny. Maybe now you understand why some genes reappear after several generations.

Sex: The sex of an organism is determined by the sex chromosomes X and Y. The name is derived from the type of chromosomes that resemble an X and a Y, respectively. Males have the chromosome pair X and Y and females the pair X and X. Apart from sex chromosomes, parakeets have other chromosome pairs. Humans, for instance, have 46 chromosomes, of which two are sex chromosomes and 22 are other pairs (= 44 chromosomes). The small difference: In parakeets, females have X- and Y-chromosomes, males only X-chromosomes. Which bird carries what sex chromosomes plays a role especially among white and yellow parakeets.

Albinos are white parakeets and Lutinos are yellow parakeets. In these birds, the color pigment melanin is absent. The gene for melanin is located on X-chromosomes and is recessive. It can happen that a Lutino female that mates with a genetically pure green male produces green progeny only—irrespective of whether these are male or female. On the other hand, if the male is heterozygous, half of the progeny are green and the other half are yellow. Anyone who is interested in this hereditary process in detail should refer to the appropriate literature (see page 141).

Important for Breeding

Breeding in parakeets generally takes place only when the pair has found a dark cave as a suitable nursery for incubating the eggs and raising the young. For that purpose, wild living parakeets in Australia search for suitable caves in old, hollow trees and branches. They do not alter the interior of the brood cave. The females gnaw along the perimeter of the entrance holes, which are usually round or oval shaped. The diameter varies from $1\frac{1}{4}$ to 2 inches (3 to 6 cm) (see tip, left). That size of a hole is optimal for parakeets, because with smaller diameters the birds have difficulties entering and leaving. However, the hole must also not be larger than that; otherwise predators or competitors for the same brood cave can endanger eggs and chicks. Your parakeets are not exposed to these sorts of dangers, and yet they still require a suitable nest box. Without it, breeding will not succeed, because females develop the hormones needed for reproduction only in the dark confines of a nest box.

TIP

Size of the entrance hole

How large the entrance hole needs to be has been closely studied. Female parakeets selected between different nest boxes, with entrance holes of the following diameters: 1 inch, 1½ inch, 2 ¼ inch (2.5 cm, 3.5 cm, and 5.5 cm). The result was clear: The ideal size is 1½ inch (3.5 cm).

▲

Mating. The male is placing his wing lovingly around the female.

Nest Box

Suitable nest boxes are available from pet shops. Make sure the one you select is of the correct size: height $5^1/_2$ inches (14 cm), width 28 inches (70 cm), and length 10 inches (24 cm). Nest boxes smaller than that are not recommended, because they offer insufficient space for the young and have inadequate air circulation, which is important for incubating eggs. The actual nest depression should not be directly underneath the entry hole, but instead off to one side, so that eggs and chicks are not inadvertently trampled on during entrance and egress. A landing perch outside the entrance hole is very important. Females tend to prefer nest boxes with a landing perch to those without a landing perch. The lid of the nest box must be hinged so that it can be opened up for easy cleaning.

Breeding in a cage: I recommend that the nest box be attached outside the cage, so that the little parrots can fully use the entire inside of the cage.
If the cage has only one door, you simply attach the box with two hooks to the outside of the cage mesh. With a pair of pliers, you remove some of the wire bars so that the bird has unimpeded access to the box. Once breeding has been completed, you simply close off the hole with a small piece of wire mesh.
Breeding in the aviary: If you want to breed with several birds in an aviary, you need to consider the following points: The distance between nest boxes must be at least 39 inches (1 m), prefer-

ably more. During nest box selection, females tend to be extremely aggressive and will attack each other, often drawing blood. In fact, there are females that sit on the landing perch constantly, threatening the incubating female on the inside. The only remedy against this is a sufficiently large distance between nest boxes. At worst, the aggressor needs to be isolated for few days in a separate cage, from which the birds can see and hear the other ones in the aviary. The Australian biologist Edmund Wynham observed among wild-living parakeets that aggression between females distinctly abated when the distance between nesting sites in the same tree was about 39 inches (1 m). Some females are rather choosy, so it is useful to offer several nest boxes. He noticed that lower nest boxes are selected only when the upper ones are already occupied. Parakeets clearly prefer boxes at higher locations.

Partner Selection, Courtship, and Mating

Wild-living parakeets cannot afford to spend a great deal of time selecting a partner, engaging in courtship rituals for days, followed by extensive nesting preparations. The time for all that simply is not there in the wild. In effect, they are virtually in the "start position" (to breed) at all times. As soon as the first raindrops fall, they have to commence their breeding activity if they want to win the race against the short rainy season. Nowadays, we have a better understanding of how these birds are able to select the "right" partner immediately from among all the other look-alike birds in the flock.

The "bride" that is being courted: The story begins with the courting male, which fluffs up its head and chest feathers, twittering in front of the selected female, pecking her beak in a demanding fashion. Sometimes the male will also feed the female, not because she is hungry, but to get her into a peaceful and receptive mood. This courtship feeding, the regurgitation of food from the crop, is also often exhibited by hand-tamed parakeets toward the owner, toward a mirror in the cage, or toward a plastic substitute bird. In effect, single males feed the human or a replacement object, respectively, as a substitute for a missing sex partner.

If a hen is benevolently inclined toward a courting male, she will extend the tail feathers up and bend her head backward. For the male this is an unmistakable sign to climb onto the back of the female and start copulating (see photograph, page 117).

What male parakeets must offer: Female parakeets prefer males with clean cheek patches. We are indebted to E. Zampiga from the Konrad Lorenz

(see photograph, page 117).

TIP

It must not be too warm

Do not place the cage with the nest box near a heater. In that location, it would be too warm and too dry. The fertilized eggs could become desiccated. A temperature-controlled, draft-free and not excessively shaded room is ideal for providing optimal breeding conditions.

The female inspects a nest box. Will she like it? ▶

Institute for this amazing discovery. Why do females select such males? Could it be that a clean plumage better reflects light? The neurobiologist Justin Marshall from the University of Queensland in Australia verified this idea when he observed that females during partner selection prefer males with fluorescent plumage.

With some clever experiments, he was able to show that the cheek feathers absorb UV light and reflect fluorescent light. Under such conditions, the small yellow feathers are shinier and radiate much more brightly. You can see a similar effect in a disco that is illuminated in blue and where the prevailing light has a high UV content. Under such conditions, white clothing radiates much more strongly. For the female parakeet, such "radiating" males are the healthier ones and make the better fathers. However, beauty is not all that is required. The ability to imitate the female's song also plays a role in partner selection (see page 108).

Finally, age is also an important factor. Young female parakeets prefer older males, although they have close social ties to other birds of their own age. Young males prefer females that have a nest box. Males are sexually mature in about 130 days after leaving the nest box, females after 112 days. I believe that sympathy and antipathy also play a role in the courtship process; however, proving that is difficult.

In spite of favorable preconditions, sometimes individually kept pairs will not get into courtship moods. The reason for that is that parakeets are social animals that need other pairs around them for stimulation.

Studies have shown that the testes and ovaries in pairs that were able to see and hear the other birds of the flock or aviary were larger than those in individually kept pairs. Testes and ovaries produce hormones that are also involved in triggering courtship behavior.

My tip: Record the twittering of parakeets, for instance, in a pet shop, and play that back to your single pair.

Healthy and Happy

Newly born parakeets are blind, naked, and weigh only 2 g, but are full of life. However, they need intensive care from their parents to survive. The mother parakeet carries the principal burden.

Male parakeets have no say when it comes to selecting the nest box. This is purely a matter for the female to decide, but its first visit to the nest box is rather short. The hen will slip in and immediately out again and then fly away.

The Time Before Hatching

During subsequent inspections she remains longer and then gnaws along the inside walls and in the depression of the floor. During this phase, the female is rather sensitive to disturbances. Therefore, you should avoid anything that could upset the bird (excessive activities in the room, loud noises) otherwise she might leave the nest box permanently, which means that she will not get into breeding mood. How does the female get into breeding mood? She needs to sit inside the nest box for a long period, listening to the song of the chosen male. Only at that point will the hormones that control breeding behavior become active. Without these hormones, nothing is going to happen.

The behavior changes dramatically after the female has laid the first eggs. At intervals of one to two days, one egg each is deposited on the unpadded floor of the nest box, until the clutch is made up of three to five eggs (sometimes even more). The female will leave the nest box only to defecate. However, she does not merely sit on the eggs for the entire duration of the incubation period. She touches the eggs with her thick tongue, turning them, and she moves the eggs continuously with her beak and so keeps changing their position. Also, the female usually picks out some of the breast or abdomen feathers to enable skin-to-egg contact. This allows her body heat to keep the eggs warm. These activities, which appear unnecessary, have an important biological purpose. They ensure an even warming of the eggs and facilitate proper gas exchange.

About 24 hours before hatching, the chick begins to chirp inside the egg. This prepares its mother for the hatching. The following, profound change is not easy for the female. Suddenly there is a naked, wiggling, living being that she has never seen before. Had the female parakeet not been prepared by the persuading, begging sounds of her progeny, she could have taken the hatchling as an intruder and attacked it. I advise against interfering in the brooding activities by cleaning remaining eggs that have been soiled by siblings that have already hatched earlier. The embryo could die because of improper handling, and the wax layer of the eggshell could be destroyed. It protects the embryo against disease pathogens.

Note: Checking the eggs to see whether they are fertile should be done only in the absence of the female. Infertile eggs can be recognized in that they are nearly totally transparent when held against a light source. Fertile eggs can be recognized in that they are darker and have a bluish sheen. Remove the infertile eggs only from a large clutch (more than four eggs), because the female can presumably recognize via the chest patches (nearly featherless areas on the chest) when the number of eggs has been substantially changed and may abandon the nest box.

Difficult "Birth"

It requires a lot of physical effort for the chick to free itself from the eggshell, something that is not always successful. Then the female has to change over from incubating to caring. From the inside, the chick breaks a tiny hole into the eggshell. It uses the "egg tooth," a small, pointed calcium projection on the upper side of the soft beak (it falls off later on), and pokes against the shell. The chick has to work hard to enter this world until it has cut a narrow crack into the shell. Finally, in a last major physical effort, the chick stretches itself and pushes half of the eggshell up. Chicks are able to push themselves out through the opening with their wings, entering the world chirping loudly.

Development of the Young

Upon hatching, young parakeets are totally naked and blind, and so weak that they are not—unlike other birds—

even able to raise their heads in the direction of the female to beg for food. The female then simply puts the chicks on their back and pushes food into their beaks; however, parakeets grow fast.

- Parakeet chicks are fledged in four weeks, and are already able to breed after another two months.
- The weight of the young increases rapidly, and at just over 1 ounce (30 g) they almost reach adult weight on their 16th or 17th day after hatching.
- On the 6th or 7th day, the eyes will open. On the 7th day the primary feathers, and on the 9th day the

This young parakeet was hand-tamed early and is therefore quite relaxed.

▼

The Development—
at a Glance

Nearly hatched ▶

A parakeet egg weighs about 2 g, and is—as with nearly all cavity brooders—white, without sheen, and with a blunt point. The embryo develops into a viable chick within 18 days.

◀ Age differences

The chicks do not hatch all at the same time, but successively. The female will always feed the youngest ones first. These juvenile birds are about two weeks old.

Soon grown up ▶

At approximately three weeks, the young will already walk about inside the nest box and start playing with each other. However, the first flying laps will not be undertaken until the birds are about four to five weeks old.

control feathers, start to grow. The down plumage will be fully developed after 11 to 12 days.

▸ After four to five weeks—at the time of leaving the nest box—the primary feathers have grown to three-fourths of their full length and the control feathers to about two thirds of their final length.

▸ The young are already adequate flyers, and it will take only another seven days until the entire plumage is fully developed.

▸ Up to the first molt (change of juvenile plumage to that of adults), the feathers of juvenile parakeets are not as shiny and strong as in adult birds.

▸ The eyes are uniformly dark and without a colored ring around the iris. The sex of the young birds cannot yet be determined by the coloration of the cere. This will change color gradually and is not fully colored until sexual maturity (see page 14).

The Chicks Are Discovering the World

While still at a delicate age, young parakeets seek contact with siblings. They will move close together, the youngest at the bottom, the older ones on top, resting neck to neck. The young will remain in that position even when the mother leaves the nest box. This provides them with warmth, softness, and an optimal resting position. On the eighth or ninth day after hatching, they are able to hold their heads up and hobble about in the nest box. After three weeks the chicks become more independent, scratching each other's sprouting feathers. At that age, playlike exploring of the surrounding area will also commence. I have often observed chicks picking up the same feather and pulling on it, like little boys pull on a rope. These are the first exercises in social behavior.

About a week before they leave the nest box, at an age of four to five weeks, they often flap their wings. They push their heads through the entrance hole to observe what is happening out there in the big wide world. After leaving the nest box, the chicks are still fed by their parents for a few days. Sometimes it happens that a young bird that had left the box already loses his courage and returns into the compound of the nest box. It is attracted by the begging sounds of its siblings in the box. Do not remove that chick from the nest box but wait until the entire batch has become fledged. **Important:** as soon as the first chick has left the box, you will need to provide food and water where the young bird can easily find it. It is advisable to place food bowls and spikes of millet at various locations in the aviary. For parakeets in a cage, scatter some food along the bottom and if you wish, give a spike of millet.

Tip: The bird hobbyist should have a cautious look inside the brood box daily to examine the condition of the chicks' feet and legs. It can happen that these appendages become encrusted with feces that later solidifies, so that the mobility of the toes is impeded and the feet become crippled. Gently clean encrusted feet with a wet cloth or a piece of paper towel. However, you should wait for a suitable opportunity when the female has left the box; otherwise she will complain loudly and possibly attack your hand.

Care of the Young

Female parakeets are very compassionate mothers. When a chick calls out and kicks its legs, it is the signal for the mother to feed. During the first few days after hatching the young are being fed at night just as frequently as during the day. The female will remain with her brood throughout the entire night—except when leaving the nest box briefly to defecate outside. Therefore, I recommend leaving a little nightlight burning, so that she can find her way back to the nest box without any problems. From approximately the eighth day onward, the chicks are rarely fed at night anymore. Even the loudest begging calls cannot persuade the mother. Obviously, she knows which ones the younger chicks are, and she will feed those first. On the other hand, the male, which frequently helps with the feeding, frequently responds to the cries of the more aggressive young. Often these are the female chicks. They tend to be given a lot more food by the male, as was observed by J. A. Stamps. This way, the females can leave the nest box earlier and achieve sexual maturity more quickly. This raises the question of supplementary feed. According to my many years of experience, parakeets do not need a special rearing diet, provided, of course, that the regular food contains all the essential nutrients. However, rearing foods cannot do any harm, so each breeder should make

MY PET

How considerate are parakeet parents?

Parakeets come into this world naked, blind, and nearly helpless. Without the intensive care of their parents they would not have a chance of surviving even for a single day. Why not check out such "paternal and maternal love."

The test begins:

During the entire breeding season, try to monitor and record daily for about half an hour, how frequently the male provides food and the female leaves the nest box. In addition, you should check how frequently both parents feed the chicks. Of course, you will not be able to see that directly, but you will hear the calling. During feeding, the chicks are begging loudly for food. You will recognize the begging sound immediately—it is unmistakable.

My test results:

A colorful little flock of birds. Anyone who breeds parakeets needs to know about genetics.

his or her own decision and act accordingly. The tasks of the mother are not confined to feeding.

She also huddles the young under her wings. During the first few days, huddling is of considerable importance, since parakeet chicks—presumably like other very young bird chicks—initially cannot maintain a constant body temperature. Therefore, the female sits on them constantly and covers them completely. However, huddling will decrease with the increasing activity of the young.

Once Breeding is Over

Parakeets do not clean out their own brood caves. In nature, ants and other insects take over this task. You will have to do that for your parakeets. Use a stiff brush and hot water, and clean out the nest box thoroughly. You should avoid all cleaning during the brood period, so that the birds are not disturbed. The nest box shouldn't be placed in the cage or in the aviary before the next desired breeding.

Time to Say Good-bye to the Young

I follow the rules of nature when it comes to parting with my young birds. Three to six days after leaving the nest box, the parents stop feeding their offspring. That, for me, is the ideal time for the separation. Some breeders start giving away the birds one to two days before they leave the nest box. I believe that is too early.

What to Do When There Are Problems

Difficulties with parakeets are frequently caused by incorrect handling of the birds or because of husbandry (care and maintenance) mistakes. Check your knowledge about these small parrots.

How to Solve Husbandry (Keeping) Problems Correctly

Once you understand the nature and requirements of your parakeets and take them fully into account, nearly nothing can go wrong. Yet, sometimes problems do arise. How to solve them is discussed in this chapter.

Most problems that come up in connection with keeping parakeets are relatively easy to solve with some attention to and understanding of your feathered housemates.

Courting the Mirror

A parakeet that is being kept as a solitary bird cannot lead a normal "parakeet life" with a partner. Anyone who has witnessed the tender billing of a pair of parakeets, can appreciate how desperately a single parakeet might look for relief from its unsatisfied innate drives. In desperation the bird courts shiny objects, such as a mirror. Although it does not recognize itself in a mirror (see page 106), it sees another parakeet in the reflection and attempts to feed it. The bird regurgitates a food mixture from his crop and rubs it onto the mirror. However, this does not provide natural relief, because courtship is a reciprocal reaction between two partners and culminates by copulation. Of course, not every courtship is followed by an actual mating, but a partner

always receives the species-correct responses. Yet, by using the mirror, the bird essentially courts . . . a vacuum. After a few months of this, the mirror-induced, misguided courtship behavior can lead to disturbances in reproductive behavior. Such a male will have difficulties mating with a female. Anyone looking for a female for such a lonely male parakeet and expecting progeny should not endanger the natural reproductive behavior with a mirror in the cage. To avoid problems with a mirror, simply

Lonely parakeets tend to court a mirror, because they think they are looking at another parakeet in the reflection.

don't put one in the cage if you're only keeping one parakeet.

Can a Single Bird Also Be Happy?

A human cannot be a replacement for another parakeet. However, a single parakeet can be kept if it is offered a lot of attention. Make sure to provide your feathered companion with enough toys and activities for mental simulation. If you put in enough effort, there is no reason why a single bird would not be happy.

The Parakeet Refuses Green Feed

Although fresh food is healthy for parakeets and must not be absent from any diet plan, some birds refuse green feed. It is very difficult to change the feeding habits especially with older birds. It is advisable to start early in the day with a diverse diet (see page 68). **My tip:** Cut the green feed into such small pieces that they can be mixed in with the seed, so that the birds feed on these pieces

coincidentally and so get a taste for green feed. Another possibility is to spread out finely cut-up green feed on your hand and try to attract the bird to it. As a rule, parakeets investigate all objects on your hand with their beak. In order to stimulate the appetite of the little parrot, you can also place a few millet seeds in your hand. With some luck, the bird will first take the seed and then the green feed.

When the Leg Has Swollen Because of the Leg Band

Wearing a leg band is not mandatory for every parakeet that is sold (see page 53). Show parakeets, however, must be banded. However, I must also add that the leg band is not completely harmless to parakeets. The bird can become entangled with it, and a subsequent struggle can lead to a broken leg. Bands that are fitted too tightly can impede blood flow. That can lead to leg amputation by a veterinarian. It is important to make sure the ring or band is fitted properly. When the leg becomes swollen, the ring must be removed.

Parakeets Mourn the Loss of Their Partners

I have no doubt that parakeets also have feelings, and most parakeet owners will agree with me. However, what exactly a parakeet is feeling is difficult to ascertain. Parakeets do not make it as easy for us, as—for instance—a dog or a cat, whose behavior is easier for us to understand. Birds do not have facial expressions and their vocalization is often alien to us. Their large relatives, the African gray parrots, express their

Single birds cannot lead a species-correct life.
▼

feelings more clearly. I can still remember very vividly a touching scene when my wife returned home from a long journey. Rocky, the name of one of my gray parrots, was unable to hide his joy. The bird emitted very soft, gentle tones, fluffed up his feathers, and approached her head, digging with his beak into her long black hair. This greeting scene usually lasted five to ten minutes. For Konrad Lorenz, the founder of behavioral biology, Nobel Prize winner, and "father" of the grey goose, there were

of a grieving gander, and noticed that during the mourning period certain hormone levels increased. This is essentially the same situation as with us when we are sad. In fact, I have also observed mourning among parakeets, although admittedly not as distinctly. One particular parakeet lived alone for years with an elderly woman. They kept each other company, and the woman

DID YOU KNOW THAT . . .

. . . a parakeet can get lost?

A parakeet that has escaped can become so disoriented that he can no longer find his way back home. Such a parakeet has usually never seen open sky before, much less different birds, houses, and trees. All these strange things frighten him. His reaction, as a fleeing animal, is instinctive. The bird flies about in panic and confusion until he has to land somewhere because of exhaustion. Usually, that is very far away from his home location.

no doubts that birds have feelings. In a very descriptive and touching essay, he describes the mourning of a grey gander, when the bird had lost its female partner. The bird appeared totally broken, without any activity, and its head was literally hanging down. Such a "widowed" goose conveys the impression of hopeless desolation. The goose lost all assertiveness and declined into apathy.

What Konrad Lorenz was able to witness can nowadays be documented with modern methods of biochemistry. Researchers studied the hematology

was extremely kind to her bird. Unfortunately, she could not be convinced that the bird needed a partner. After she died, the parakeet was given to her daughter. Initially the bird was listless, and hardly ever sang or moved about. Eventually, the bird started to cheer up slightly, but its behavior remained reserved. An attempt to provide a partner failed. The bird remained in its apathy. Although I have seen that a remaining parakeet, upon the death of its partner, calls out for its partner, I had never seen behavior like that. Yet, one should attempt to provide a new partner for the surviving bird. There does not seem to be any doubt that parakeets can feel emotional pain. They display their pain with loud screeching. That can always be witnessed when the birds are fighting, and when one attacks the other somewhat roughly. From what we know now about the feelings of animals, it would be senseless to deny similar emotions to parakeets. I have also seen how tender and caring these birds can be toward each other.

When the Parakeets Are Getting Old

Signs of old age occur not only among people, but also in animals. This is easier to notice in dogs and cats than in birds. However, when you look closely at your aging male or female parakeet, you can also see distinct evidence of advancing old age. In males, the blue cere often turns brownish as the years go by. That is a sign of hormonal changes. In addition, the flying skill of these (normally) clever flyers tends to diminish. Fortunately, this happens only during the final months of their lives. Although it is the proverbial "piece of cake" for your parakeets to fly around obstacles, that becomes increasingly difficult for older birds. Older parakeets prefer short, straight flight paths so that they can better manage their physical strength. Older parakeets, much like older people, also need familiar surroundings. Food and water bowls should always be at the same, easily reachable location. Slightly slower and more awkward movements suggest an older bird. The bond between the partners of a pair remains intact, even when one of the partners is many years younger. Apparently, the age difference does not separate the birds. The food and feeding behavior rarely change in older age. Similarly, the preferences for particular foods remain, except that the birds are feeding less on green feed. What is conspicuous, though, is

▶ *There can be physical disagreements when the best place at a tasty spike of millet is at stake.*

Before acquiring your parakeets, you must inform yourself about their **nature and requirements**. Only after you have done that are there no obstacles in the path to a happy human-to-animal relationship.

that older birds vocalize less, presumably under the motto *I must now save my energy*. According to my observations, very old birds do not change their plumage as often; some may not do it anymore at all. There are virtually no typical old-age diseases among parakeets, except the development of tumors.

The Parakeet Mother Has Died

Unfortunately, it can happen that the parakeet mother dies while she is rearing young. In most cases, the young will die unless it is possible to find a foster mother for them. If you (or an acquaintance parakeet owner) happen to have a female that is just rearing young, the chances are quite good that she can rear the orphaned chicks at the same time. Fortunately, female parakeets will accept chicks of a different age from another clutch, and care for them like their own.

The female has no problems adjusting to the age of orphaned chicks. For instance, if she has five-day-old chicks from another clutch and three-week-old chicks of her own in the same nest box, she will feed the very young ones at night as well, while no longer feeding the older ones. It would be ideal, of course, if you could find a female with young that are about the same age for

the orphans. If such a female can be found, there are no problems. When the added chicks are much younger than those already with the female, there is a danger that the little ones will not be sufficiently fed, because the feeding activities by the female naturally diminish as her chicks grow.

Raising orphaned parakeets "by hand" is more complicated than one might think. In fact, for chicks that are only a few days old, this is extremely difficult. And one should only do so after being properly trained. It is not for beginners. They require special commercially prepared formulas. Hand-rearing food is essentially a powder that is mixed into a mash. Additional complications arise from the fact that the little birds need to be fed four to five times a night.

Food syringes are usually too large. One needs a special syringe available from a veterinarian. Even with older birds, hand rearing is not easy.

Intruders in the Nest Box

If there are several pairs in an aviary that are breeding simultaneously, any mother—just as in the wild—will vehemently defend her brood against invaders. For instance, if another female looks through the entrance hole into the nest box, the mother reacts instantly by aggressively hacking that female.

▶ *Crash landings can also happen to parakeets.*

breeding attempts no longer display this behavior.

Getting Used to Each Other

Parakeets are flock birds, and a characteristic of flocks is that some birds will leave the flock and new ones will join it. Consequently, it is no problem at all to add another parakeet to a small group of birds in an aviary. It becomes far more difficult when one bird from a bonded pair dies and you want to provide a new partner for the remaining bird. In such a case it can happen that the remaining bird considers a new one to be an intruder and attacks it. To prevent this you need to accustom the birds to each other gradually. This gives the old bird an opportunity to grieve and at the same time, get used to the newcomer gradually.

Place two cages side by side, so that the parakeets can hear and see each other. Initially, there should be a distance between the cages, but you can reduce that gradually over the next few hours. The next day you can put the cages directly side by side, so that the birds can establish contact through the wires. After this period of adjustment (two to three days) I let the birds fly together. Upon completion of this exploratory tour and the mutual physical contact, it is back into their respective cages. You should repeat this procedure two or three times. In all likelihood, the birds are then getting along without any problems.

If that bird does not retreat immediately, a fight can erupt that can lead to serious injuries. If the mother does not defend her chicks, the rival female could kill them. There are female parakeets that go virtually berserk. In fact, some females move from one nest box to the next, threatening the incubating mothers. At the first opportunity, they slip into the box and kill all the chicks. Why these females act the way they do, I do not understand nor do I know the reason. One thing is certain though: Such a female must be removed from the aviary immediately. You could try mating such a troublemaker with a male in a separate cage. I have seen it happen that such females in subsequent

"Perpetual Breeders"

Two broods per year are sufficient for female parakeets; otherwise, the danger arises that they will die of exhaustion. Unfortunately, the female parakeets will not stop breeding on their own, and to prevent them from continued breeding is not easy. Presumably, this reproductive drive is part of the genetic makeup, because their wild cousins are breeding continuously when there are optimal environmental conditions. As pet birds, parakeets are always under optimal environmental conditions. There is sufficient food and drink. To stop the birds from reproducing is difficult, and the only available possibility is certainly not in line with accepted animal welfare practices. On the other hand, this measure could save the life of the female. Separate the parakeet pair just before the chicks leave the nest box. Accommodate the birds for four to five days in separate rooms. This way the female is no longer stimulated by the male to

TIP

Hand-reared birds

Hand-raised chicks are usually sweet and tame and take readily to human companionship. It is generally advised to look for hand-raised baby birds, and to never purchase unweaned chicks. When not being handled or hand-fed, the chicks benefit from being around their parents and siblings. The chicks should not be totally pulled from their parents and siblings because it can have an adverse effect on their development.

breed (see page 132). However, if the female has already started laying eggs again—which is very likely—permit the hen to lay all her eggs.

Learning to "Talk"

It is a highlight for every parakeet owner when his bird finally begins to talk. Unfortunately, the reason for that is often of a somewhat sad nature: Talking parakeets are often very lonely birds that are trying to establish contact this way. The reverse of this occurs among parakeets that live together in a flock. They speak generally only the "parakeet language." However, parakeets are personalities, and as such, they all have different characters and traits.

At the University of Arizona, in Tucson, I have seen how three male "speech geniuses" spoke several words and short sentences although they lived in a small flock. However, they were separated daily for two hours from the flock and given individual speech instructions by a trainer. The birds were given a tasty treat as soon as they mimicked something correctly. With a lot of understanding and patience it may be possible to have paired parakeets as well as those living in groups talking.

Your Parakeet Has Escaped

A bird that has escaped and does not know its surroundings will not be able to return home unaided. Such a bird's chances are improved when it is tame and has already seen its surroundings frequently.

My tip: Take the cage with your parakeets occasionally outside onto the balcony or into the garden when the

MY PET

How do parakeets spend their day?

Become a behavioral scientist for a day to find out what your parakeets are doing all day long. At certain times of the day check whether your birds are resting, or whether they are active or particularly sociable.

The test begins:

Record the behavior of a single parakeet six times within the course of the day. Confine yourself to a specific bird. Observing several parakeets at the same time is too difficult and would provide inaccurate results. Draw up a table where you record what the bird is doing. Better yet, document the behavior with a video camera if you can. Of course, you can also spread your research activities over several days.

My test results:

weather is good. Be aware of cats and birds of prey! This way your birds will gradually become accustomed to traffic noise, strange birds, and animals. They need to learn what their environment looks like.

Punky, one of my male parakeets found an open window one evening. Curious as he was, he flew outside. However, after flying a few laps around our house, the bird settled on our neighbor's television antenna. From there he called out in full voice. I grabbed the cage and climbed onto the roof. With a single hop, the bird returned to his secure home. Never attempt to catch a bird with your hand, but instead always use the cage for recapturing the bird, so that the relationship of trust is not endangered.

Parakeets are elegant, aerial acrobats that need to be given an opportunity to fly a few laps every day. ▶

Pet-sitter Checklist

You would like to go on vacation and have a pet sitter looking after your birds. Here you can write down everything your vacation substitute will need to know. This way your parakeets are properly looked after and you can fully enjoy your trip.

My parakeets are called:

This is what they look like:

This is what they like to eat:

In these daily amounts:

Once a week in this amount:

Tasty treats for in between:

This is what they drink:

The correct feeding times:

Their food is stored at:

Cage cleaning:

Daily cleaning:

Weekly cleaning:

These are the games they like to play:

Activities to keep the birds busy:

Their intense dislikes:

My birds are not allowed to:

This is also very important:

This is their veterinarian:

My vacation address and telephone number is:

INDEX

 A

abscesses, 92
acrobatics, 108–109, 135
age, 12, 55, 130–131
alarm call, 22
American Budgerigar Society, 141
ancestors, 7–9
animal shelter, 53
aviary
  cleaning, 83, 85
  furnishings, 46
  landing site, 46
  outdoor, 43–45

 B

balancing act, 12
ball rolls, 12
bathing, 82
beak, 19, **81–83**
beak-grinding stone, 41, 52
beauty contest, 27
behavior, 13, 22, 24, 53
bells, 98
billing, 20, 23
biological profile, 11–13
birdbath, 40
birth, 121
bleeding wounds, 95
body
  language, 22–24
  temperature, 12
  weight, 11–12
bonding, 19–20, 22, 58, 122, **132**
books on parakeets, 141
boredom, 35, 97, **99–100**
bottom tray, 39
brain, 106–107
breeders, 51–52, 57, **133**

breeding, 21, 116–120
breeding stock, 113–114
budding leaves, 74
Budgerigar Association of America, 141

 C

cage
  bottom tray, 39
  disinfecting, 95
  dispenser, 40–41, 46, 67
  door, 38, 65
  furnishings, 39–42
  liners, 40
  location, 36–38
  maintenance, 44, 83
  perches, 39, 44, 46, 58
  playground, 44, 99
  size, 35, 38
  temperature, 43–44
  toys, 40, 42, 46, 48, 51, **104,** 126
  training, 44
  wire, 38
captive-bred birds, 15
cere, 52, 55
chick
  care of, 54, 124–125
  development, 121–123
  hand-raised, 133
  leaving nest, 125
  orphaned, 131
children, 11, 54–55, 64
chirping, 22, 24
claw trimming, 39, 82, **82–83,** 94
cleanliness
  cage care, 44, 83
  caring for birds, 82–83
  cleaning aviary, 83, 85
  preening, 20, **22–24,** 81–82
climbing rope, 51, 99, 104
cloaca, 13, 52, 95

clubs and organizations, 141
cocks, 8, 25, 55, 119
color recognition, 16, 103
color varieties
  cinnamon light green, 33
  cinnamon opaline dark green, 29
  dark blue, 30
  fallow dark blue, 30
  gray green, 31
  gray yellow white, 30
  light green, 31
  light-winged yellow-faced opaline, 28
  light-winged olive green, 31
  opaline spangle blue, 28
  opaline violet, 32
  rainbow, 28
  recessive pied olive green, 32
  recessive pied yellow-faced mauve, 29
  white dark blue, 30
companion bird, 24–25, 60, 97
contact call, 22
cooperation, 21
copulation, 20
corneal infection, 55
courting a mirror, 127–128
courtship, 22, 118–119, 127
creative thinking, 110–111
crop, 13, 91
curiosity, 48, 61
cuttlebone, 41, 52

 D

death, 84
diarrhea, 91–93
dietary plan, 67, 69
digestive system, 13
diseases, 87–88
DNA, 114–116
drafts, 37
droppings, 49, 52

ears, 17, 67
egg binding, 95
eggs, 19, 117, 120–122
empathy, 56
entrance hole, 116
escaped bird, 133–134
estrus, 15
eyes, 15–16, 52, 55

feather diseases, 88–90
fecal material, 81, 85, 88
feeding, 44, 131
feet and toes, 52
female birds, 14, 25, 40, 67, 119
first aid kit, 93
flocks, 7–9, 19–20, 64
food. *See also* nutrition
  dangerous, 18, **77, 79**
  deficiency, 76
  dietary plan, 67, 69
  dispenser, 40–41, 46
  fruit, 67, 71, **74,** 77–78
  green feed, 67, 74, **76,**
    77–78, 126
  nibbling, 19, 48, **78**
  preferences, 78
  requirement, 68
  searching, 102–103
  seeds, **69–71,** 74, 77
  spicy, 77
  spray millet, 58, 61–62, 74,
    78–79
  treats, 71, 77
  vegetables, 67, 71, **74,**
    76–78, 91
foraging, 39, 102–103
foxtail millet, 58, 65
free-flight, 35–36, 38, 43,
  46–48. *See also* winging
  disorder

French molt, 90
fruit, 67, 71, **74,** 77–78

games, 98–99
Going Light Syndrome (GLS),
  91–92
Gould, John, 9–10
green feed, 67, 74, **76,** 77–78,
  126
grooming, 12, 52

Hamilton & District Budgerigar
  Society Inc., 141
hand-rearing, 133
hatching, 120, 122
health signs, 52
hearing, 17
heart, 12, 87
heat lamp, 88, 93
hormonal changes, 130
human bonding, 20, 25, 60, 63
human companion, 11, 25
husbandry, 127–134
hygiene, 81

illness, 87–88
imitation, 109–110. *See also*
  mimicking
immune system, 24
intelligence, 45, 105, 110

juvenile birds, 14, 21, 55, 68

ladder, 51

landing site, 46
lattice ball, 98, 104
learning, 100–104
leg band, 53, 126
lettuce, 76
lice, 89
lid test, 45, 103
lifespan, 84
loneliness, 56, 127–128

male birds, 8, 25, 55, 119
marbles, 98
medications, 93
memory, 106
mental stimulation, 126
metabolic rate, 87
millet, 61–62, 74, **78–79**
mimicking, 17, 22, 61, **133.**
  See also imitation
minerals, 19, 74
mites, 88–89
molting, **85–86,** 91
mother, death of, 131
musculature, 12

nasal secretion, 52, 93
natural fiber threads, 104
nest box, 117–118
nest box intruder, 131–132
new home, 58–60
new partner, 132
nibbling, 19, 48, **78**
noise, 16–17, 58–59
nostrils, 52, 55
nutrition. *See also* food
  carbohydrates, 72–73
  deficiency, 76
  dietary plan, 68–71, **74**
  fats, 73
  minerals, 74

preferences, 18
protein, 72
supplying, 59
vitamins, 75–76

obesity, 67, 70. *See also*
  slimming
old age, 130–131
oviduct, 95

paint, non-toxic, 98
painting, 45
pair bonding, 19–20, 22, 112,
  132
pair compatibility, 25
paper balls, 104
parakeets
  age to purchase, 55
  classification of, 25–26
  color varieties, 27–33
  cost of, 10
  domesticated, 22, 24
  as food, 10
  homosexual, 25
  in new home, 58–60
  as pets, 9–10
  purchasing, 55
parrot disease, 53, 91
partner, loss of, 126–130
pasta, uncooked, 98, 104
pecking order, 20
pedigree breeding, 55
pencil game, 99
perches, 39, 44, 46, 58
personality, 60, 101
pets, other, 37, 64
pet shop, 52
pet sitter, 94, 136–137
playground, 42, **99**
playing, 40, 97

plumage
  adult, 21
  grooming, 7, 94–95
  healthy, 52
  molting, 85–86
preen (oil) gland, 22
preening, 20, **22–24,** 81–82
progeny, 113
psittacine beak and feather
  disease (PBFD), 90

rain shower, 9
recognition, 105–106
respiratory system, 12–13
rewards, 101

Schnegg, Antoine, 69
screeching, 22
searching for food, 102–103
seed dispenser, 40
seeds, 69–71, **74,** 77
sensory capabilities, 14–15
sexing birds, 14
show standards, 27
sickness, 87–88
single bird, 126
size, 15
skeleton, 11
skin diseases, 88–90
skin fungi, 89–90
sleeping, 23, 65
slimming, 68–69
smell, 17–18
solitary birds, 24
songs, 22
species-survival instinct, 21
spray millet, 58, 61–62, 74,
  78–79
stress, 52, 56
study program, 107

swing, 51, 99, 104

taming, 61–63
taste, 18
temperature, 43–44
testes, 21, 119
threatening posture, 23
toxic and dangerous, 18, **77, 79**
toys, 40, 42, 46, 48, 51, **104,**
  126
transport box, 57–58
treats, 71, 77
tree climbing, 48–49
Trillmich, Fritz, 19
Tri-State Budgerigar Society,
  141
tumors, 92, 131
twittering, 65

vacation, 94
vegetables, 67, 71, **74,** 76, 78,
  91
ventilation, 13, 37
veterinarian, 80, 87–88
vibration, 18, 37
viral diseases, 90–92
vocalization, 24, 108–109

water, 9, 77, **79**
  dispenser, 40–41, 46, 67
weight, 15, 86
wild birds, 15
wild plants, 76
wing flapping, 24
winging disorder, 46–47. *See
  also* free-flight
World Budgerigar Association,
  27

RESOURCES

Clubs and Organizations

Budgerigar Association of America
www.budgerigarassociation.com

The American Budgerigar Society
www.abs1.org

Tri-State Budgerigar Society
www.tri-statebudgie.org

Western Canada Budgerigar Association
http://web.mac.com/idealinbudgies/iWeb/abcWcba/abcWcba.html

Hamilton & District Budgerigar Society Inc.
http://www3.sympatico.ca/davehansen/index.html

Books

Freud, Arthur. 1999. *Parakeets, A Complete Owner's Manual.* Hauppauge, NY: Barron's Educational Series, Inc.

Niemann, Hildegard. 2008. *Budgerigars, A Complete Owner's Manual.* Hauppauge, NY: Barron's Educational Series, Inc.

Wolter, Annette and Monika Wegler. 1994. *The Complete Book of Parakeet Care.* Hauppauge, NY: Barron's Educational Series, Inc.

Viner, Bradley, B. Vet Med, MRCVS. *All About Your Budgerigar.* Hauppauge, NY: Barron's Educational Series, Inc.

Magazines/Journals

Bird Talk
P.O. Box 6050
Mission Viejo, CA 92690-6050
www.birdchannel.com/bird-magazines/bird-talk/default.aspx

Birds USA
www.birdchannel.com/bird-magazines/birds-usa/busa-2009/birds-usa.aspx

Budgies (Popular Birds Series)
http://www.birdchannel.com/bird-magazines/popular-birds/budgies.aspx

Budgerigar Journal
624 West 9th Street, Suite 100
San Pedro, California 90731
http://www.budgerigarassociation.com/baa_020.htm

USEFUL WEBSITES

Links from Hamilton & District Budgerigar Society Inc.
www3.sympatico.ca/davehansen/links.html

General Parakeet Information
www.cuteducky.com/cute_animals/keet.html

"Let's Talk Birds"
www.letstalkbirds.com/budgie.htm

Parakeet Training Care
www.lisashea.com/petinfo/budgie.html

Animal World: "Parakeet Families"
http://animal-world.com/encyclo/birds/parakeets/parakeets.htm

Parakeet Care, Raising Parakeets, Parakeet Age, and More
www.yellowyorkie.com/parakeet-care.php

Parakeet Health
*www.pet-parrots.com/Parakeets/
parakeet-health.html*

Answers about parakeets are also available from your local pet shop or parakeet breeder (especially the latter if that was the source of your birds). Beyond that, a vast amount of parakeet husbandry (maintenance and care) information is available free of change on the Internet. Search for "how to keep parakeets."

ACKNOWLEDGMENTS

I would like to thank my doctorate mentor, Professor Tschanz, with whom I have had many constructive discussions—often well into the night—on the behavior of parakeets, and also express my gratitude to Professor A. Steiger for his practical parakeet research.

PHOTOGRAPHS

Illustrations of opening chapter pages:
Page 6: Parakeets will gnaw on anything.
Page 34: Mutual nibbling of each other's plumage
Page 50: Soft landing.
Page 66: Millet tastes wonderful.
Page 80: Taking care of the plumage.
Page 96: Exercising on the cloth.
Page 112: Billing.
Page 126: Harmless nibbling fun.

Photographers

Oliver Giel is a specialist nature and animal photographer. Together with his life partner, Eva Scherer, he is involved with pictorial productions for books, magazines, calendars and advertising. For further details about his photographic studio visit *www.tierfotograph.com.*

Monika Wegler is among the best pet photographers in Europe. She is also successful as a journalist and animal-book author. Many of her books have been published by Gräfe und Unzer Verlag. For further details about her work see *www.wegler.de.* She has provided the following photographs for this pet guide: Cover 3-3, 5-bottom, 6, 17 – top, 23-top, 28-1 round, 28-2 bottom, 29-3 top, 29-4 top-round, 29-5 bottom, 29-6 bottom-round, 30-1 top, 30-3-top-round, 30-3 bottom, 31-1 top, 31-2, top-round, 31-3-bottom, 31-4-bottom-round, 32-1-top-round, 32-2-top, 32-3-bottom, 32-4 bottom-round, 33-1-top, 33-2 bottom-round, 33-3-bottom, 34, 35-bottom, 43 top-round, 49 top, 51-bottom, 53 top, 54, 56-round, 58-1-top, 58-2-top, 59-3-top, 60, 66, 67-bottom, 69, 76-bottom, 79-bottom, 84, 85, 96, 97-bottom, 100, 104, 106-bottom, 108-1-left, 109-2-center, 109-3-right, 111-bottom, 112, 120, 122-1-left, 122-2-right, 122-3-left, 122-4-right, 122-5-left, 122-6-right, 125-top, 126, 127-bottom, 132-top, 135, Cover 5-1, U5-2, U6-1, Poster

Photographs from other photographers: Ardea: Hans & Judy Beste: 8-1, Don Hadden: 8-2, NHPA: Dave Watts: 9, Okapia: 26-bottom, Vogelzucht Arkos: 44, Weidenmüller: 45-1 & 2, Arco: 55, 113, Nature Picture Library: 115

Barron's is the best source for small animal pet owners!

> **Living with a House Rabbit**
ISBN-13: 978-0-7641-5819-3

> **Training Your Pet Rat**
ISBN-13: 978-0-7641-1208-9

> **All About Your Hamster**
ISBN-13: 978-0-7641-1014-6

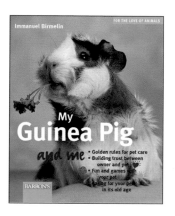

> **My Guinea Pig and Me**
ISBN-13: 978-0-7641-1806-7

> **The Ferret Handbook**
ISBN-13: 978-0-7641-1323-9

> **Gerbils**
ISBN-13: 978-0-7641-0939-3

Please visit **www.barronseduc.com** to view current prices and to order books

Barron's Educational Series, Inc.
250 Wireless Blvd.
Hauppauge, NY 11788
Order toll-free: 1-800-645-3476
Order by fax: 1-631-434-3217

In Canada:
Georgetown Book Warehouse
34 Armstrong Ave.
Georgetown, Ont. L7G 4R9
Canadian orders: 1-800-247-7160
Fax in Canada: 1-800-887-1594

(151) R 2/09

The Author

Behavioral biologist Dr. Immanuel Birmelin of Freiburg, Germany has been involved with research into the behavior of pets, and zoo and circus animals for more than 25 years. He keeps parakeets, guinea pigs, and dogs. In his doctoral dissertation, he investigated the hatching behavior of parakeets. Gräfe und Unzer Verlag has already published his GU pet guides *Parakeets*, *Happy and Healthy*, *My Guinea Pig*, *Guinea Pigs*, and *The Clever Dog*. Together with Volker Arzt, Dr. Birmelin is also the writer of many television shows about animals.

First edition for the United States, its territories and dependencies and Canada published in 2009 by Barron's Educational Series, Inc.

Published originally under the title *mein Wellensittich*, in the series *mein Heimtier*
©2008 by Gräfe und Unzer Verlag GmbH, München

English translation copyright © 2009 by Barron's Educational Series, Inc.
German edition by: Immanuel Birmelin

English translation by U. Erich Friese

All inquiries should be addressed to:
Barron's Educational Series, Inc.
250 Wireless Boulevard
Hauppauge, NY 11788
www.barronseduc.com

ISBN-10: 0-7641-4283-6
ISBN-13: 978-0-7641-4283-3

Library of Congress Cataloging-in-Publication Data

Birmelin, I. (Immanuel)
 [Mein Heimtier mein Wellensittich. English]
 Parakeet/ Immanuel Birmelin.
  p. cm – (My pet)
 Includes index.
 ISBN-13: 978-0-7641-4283-3
 ISBN-10: 0-7641-4283-6
 1. Budgerigar. I. Title
 SF473.B8B57135 2009
 636.6'865—dc22   2009005294

Printed in China
9 8 7 6 5 4 3 2 1